DOCUMEN[']
HISTORY O.[HOUSES]

N. W. Alcock

British Records Association

Archives and the User No. 10

2003

In memory of
Maurice Barley
who first showed me how to
combine houses with documents

The right of N W Alcock to be identified as author of this work has been asserted
by him in accordance with the Copyright, Designs and Patent Act, 1988

ISBN 0 900222 14 X

Printed in Great Britain by Warwick Printing Co Ltd,
Caswell Road, Leamington Spa CV31 1QD

Contents

List of Figures and Tables

FIGURES

TABLES

Abbreviations

BCA	Birmingham City Archives (formerly Birmingham Reference Library)
CRO	County Record Office
IGI	International Genealogical Index (see Further Reading)
PRO	National Archives, Public Record Office
RO	Record Office
SBTRO	Shakespeare Birthplace Trust Record Office, Stratford-upon-Avon
WCRO	Warwickshire County Record Office, Warwick

Preface

In recent years, enthusiasm for 'house history' has grown apace, encouraged by such television programmes as *The House Detectives*. As a guide to researchers in this field, John Harvey's long out of print *Sources for the History of Houses* (BRA, 1974) remains highly regarded and frequently cited. Although a reprint or revised edition of Harvey's book might have been undertaken, since it was written a number of new sources have become accessible. The emphasis of research on houses is also changing, particularly towards discovering more about the people living in a house and their circumstances – similar research to that undertaken by family historians, but given a rather different slant. For these reasons, the present volume is not a new edition of Harvey's classic but is a completely new text, though of course covering much of the same material; the case studies are drawn from my own experience. A topic that Harvey did not cover is also included, the historical development of housing and houses in general, rather than the history of specific buildings. Like its predecessor, the book is intended primarily for the interested amateur, especially the house-owner researching his own house. I hope also that it will be useful to archivists needing to advise researchers especially in relation to sources not in local record offices.

In 1974, Harvey's book stood essentially alone but now a number of guides to sources for house history do exist. Many record offices have prepared guidance leaflets for their visitors (some also being presented on the web). As well as their information about generally available sources, these are particularly useful in high-lighting the specific records for particular areas. A short guide by David Iredale and John Barratt, *Discovering your old house* (Shire, 2002) is useful, as it discusses both the physical structure of the house and the use of documentary evidence. Most other books on house history (see Further Reading) tend to concentrate on architectural developments and discuss documentary sources only in general terms.

Nick Barratt, *Tracing the history of your house* (PRO, 2001) is excellent for what it contains and is referred to below when appropriate, but its title does not make clear that it is limited almost entirely to sources in the Public Record Office, which is not where most of the materials for house history are located. Following its advice on either title deeds or law suits, unless a clue already points in that direction, is likely to involve the researcher in very laborious searches which will almost certainly be fruitless. The PRO sources need to be approached with a critical appraisal of their possible value and the balance between this and the effort required to use them, that the beginner cannot provide. The more recent book by the same author, *House History Starter Pack* (PRO, 2002), though concise, provides a good summary, including check-sheets to guide the progress of the research.

The present book is underpinned by hard-earned experience gained from the house histories I have myself researched. To an extent, therefore, it reflects the bias of these studies towards early rural houses (especially in Warwickshire) rather than, say, nineteenth or twentieth century urban houses – though I have looked at some of these.

However, the principles are the same, whatever the date of the house, even if the evidence varies. The specific documents cited relate to England and Wales. Property law was different in Scotland and so other sources need to be used, which are outside the scope of this book. For Northern Ireland and Eire, although the legal framework was the same as in England, the survival of records is very patchy and local guidance will also be needed.[1]

Acknowledgements I should thank especially the many house-owners whose houses I have studied. Without the access to their houses and their documents, this guide could never have been written. The help of Mairi Macdonald, general editor of the British Records Association has been invaluable. The staff of the many record offices I have used have also been unfailingly helpful in sharing their expertise with me.

---

[1]   For Scotland, a starting point is the factsheet *Buildings*, prepared by the National Archives of Scotland and available on their website (*http://www.nas.gov.uk/family_history_factsheet.htm*). No specific guide has been published for house history in Ireland but most general texts mention this topic briefly.

1. Introduction

Anyone researching their own or another house will probably find themselves working through the stages represented by the following five chapters of this book, approximately in the order they are set out. The starting point will almost always be the house itself. In chapter 2, the key questions to be asked of the house itself are indicated:

How old is the house?

What alterations have been made to it since it was built?

Their answers will direct the thrust of the documentary research. It is obvious but must not be forgotten that the whole approach to the sources is different for, say, a mid-nineteenth century London terrace house and a medieval Devon farm. Identifying the likely builder of a village house and discovering how it was lived in depends on knowing in advance when it was built (roughly or precisely). Furthermore, a major part of researching the history of a house involves analysing its physical structure and the changes it has undergone since it was built. In emphasising documentary sources, this book can only indicate some approaches to this essential first stage.

Turning to documentary sources, some of the questions to be answered are

Who built it – the owner when it was built, and perhaps the actual builder?

Who owned it and who lived in it?

What was its relationship to the other houses in the community? Was it the manor house, a cottage, the school, etc.)?

How was it lived in?

In answering these questions, the first need is for maps to establish the location of the house and any associated land, and its ownership at a particular date – or more than one date if possible. A particular emphasis is placed on the use of the 1909-10 'Domesday' maps and valuations – a source that can probably be used even if all others fail. Next comes evidence for the sequence of owners and tenants, initially constructed for as long a period as possible from the obvious sources. Adding to and amplifying this will be a continuing task as the research progresses. Once some information about the owners and occupiers has been gleaned, it will be possible to search out and recognise direct evidence for the house's history, especially from title deeds, manor court rolls and estate records. Lastly comes the exploration in greater depth of the people who once made the house their home, their lifestyles and social context. To a large extent, telling their story is a form of family history and uses the same sources as do family historians, with the difference that their home is already known. However, knowing the physical structure of the house itself opens up other resources for re-creating their past and how they lived and worked.

The final general chapter, that on the History of Housing, is directed to a rather different audience. It examines the type of evidence useful to those whose interests are in buildings and in their social and economic implications, rather than in studying a specific house. Here, I have tried to identify the types of information that can be found if one is either lucky or very hard-working in searching it out. A number of valuable published studies indicate especially how building evidence can be related to wider themes in history,[1] though it remains regrettably true that main-stream historians too often regard houses as no more than stage-settings, rather than as key economic evidence. Historically, then as now, a house was the largest and most expensive object that most people ever owned or used.

Inevitably, the discussion of sources within one or another of the chapters is not clear-cut. Thus, the 1910 'Domesday' Field Books identify owners and tenants, but they also describe the house. Wills identify the descent of property from one owner to another, but they often also inform us about rooms and their contents. While trying to avoid duplication, I have mentioned aspects of sources where they are relevant, even if they are discussed in more detail elsewhere.

A group of case-studies is given in the final section of the book, chosen to illustrate different aspects of evidence for houses – of course they are all success stories! They include a Victorian house (Case study 3), showing that a house built in the nineteenth century has a history, as much as a Tudor manor house or a medieval timber-framed cottage. The aspects to be researched differ with the period, but the principles are the same. Another study takes the history of a Warwickshire farmhouse back to the medieval period (Case study 2). A section in Chapter 5 examines medieval sources specifically, but it is important to emphasise that the sort of documents which can be used to identify sequences of owners and tenants at later periods rarely exist before about 1550. The best chances for success will be for houses of relatively high status such as manor houses or rectories, for houses in well-documented towns, such as Ludlow or Coventry, or for copyhold properties where the court rolls have survived (as in this case study).

One warning should be given to those starting to research their home. The detailed listing and indexing of documents in local record offices is far from perfect and many indexes will do no more than locate documents relating to particular places. In most of the house histories that I have researched, I have needed to look at almost every document that has survived for the parish in question, because I could not tell in advance which would be useful. The effort has been considerable, but the reward has been the discovery of nuggets of information that would otherwise never have come to light.

Researchers, whatever their objectives, need to be aware that they will need certain skills, though these will depend both on the type and the progress of the research. The further back the research extends, the more demanding these skills become. Palaeography will be needed for documents before about 1700 and, indeed, even later documents can set handwriting puzzles. At about the same date, Latin may be encountered, especially in manorial documents; fortunately, both its vocabulary and grammar tend to be very simple and formulaic.[2] The legal complexities of title deeds of any date can cause beginners some problems. The present text does not offer direct guidance on acquiring expertise in these fields, but some basic guides are listed in the Further Reading. It is also worth emphasising that one of the most effective ways to learn such skills is to practice them, even if guidance is needed while taking the first steps.

---

[1]   For studies of the historical and economic significance of houses see, for example, Christopher Dyer, *Standards of living in the later Middle Ages*, Cambridge University Press, 1989 and Maurice Barley, *Houses and history*, Faber and Faber, 1986.

[2]   Quotations from Latin texts have been translated, while those from English texts have been edited to remove legal repetitions, while attempting to preserve the wording and spelling of the originals.

2. The House itself

It may be unexpected for a book on the documentary history of houses to start with a discussion of their physical structure. In reality, knowing the type of house is an essential pre-requisite to deciding what sort of documents may be significant. The history of houses as objects is an immense subject on which much research has been undertaken, but as background to documentary research, the questions considered below cover the most significant aspects.

How old is the House?
Of course, many people start researching the history of their house to answer this very question. But, in reality, before you can begin studying documents in earnest it is essential to have at least a preliminary idea of the answer to this and the related question: *Is the house probably the first on the site?*

Enormous numbers of houses are parts of speculative developments in cities and towns, whether London or Frome in the seventeenth century, Bath or Leeds in the eighteenth, Leamington Spa or Salford in the nineteenth, Letchworth or Milton Keynes in the twentieth century.[1] In such towns, whole streets will share broadly the same history, making the location of relevant sources much easier. Sometimes indeed the basic research may have been done, for example by the *Survey of London*. The houses were probably built on new sites, so research on their 'pre-history' will need to examine the estate or the fields on which the new houses were laid out and the reasons for the development taking place when and where it did – questions which the researcher interested in a particular house may or may not want to explore.

Houses in the centres of towns, in villages or on isolated farm sites are much less likely to be the first on their site. Thus, the approximate date of the house is important to define the period on which the research should concentrate. More important and in contrast to houses in new developments, even the most extensive documentary evidence rarely identifies the building date, so this has to be established from the structure of the house. General clues to the dating of houses can be found by comparison with the examples given in such books as: Edmund Gray, *The British house: a concise architectural history*, Anthony Quiney, *House and home: a history of the small English house*, Maurice Barley, *The English farmhouse and cottage*, or Eric Mercer, *English Vernacular Houses*. However, it is important to look at local examples, because building techniques and designs vary greatly from region to region. Thus, if descriptions of buildings in your area have been published, this is probably the first place to search.[2] In suitable cases, tree-ring dating may be able to give an exact date for the construction of a house – or at least the date when the trees used in it were felled.[3]

The house itself is often the only source for its early history. Even if documents survive abundantly, identifying those relating to particular houses in villages is often very difficult. Houses in towns can often be recognised more easily because descriptions are generally more detailed, and some remarkable sequences of documents have been established.[4] Best of all, perhaps, are isolated farms with their own names, for which very long histories can sometimes be constructed.[5] For these houses, the date of the existing structure is crucial in deciding which documents are most relevant.

A further question which can usually only be answered by a study of the structure of the house is:

What alterations have been made to the house since it was built?

Disentangling even minor changes will help reveal the original design, but some changes are particularly significant for the developing lifestyles in the house. For medieval houses, the insertion of a chimney and an upper floor in the open hall is a key change. Regional trends can often be seen, such as the addition of lean-to dairies to many small Devon farmhouses. Many village farmhouses were extended and divided into cottages in the nineteenth century following the selling off of their farmland; more recently, re-conversion to a single dwelling is a typical change.

Architectural study of ordinary houses is more like archaeology than the style-based architectural or art history applied to understand the design links of grand country houses. It builds much more on the logic of how a timber-frame or roof structure must have fitted together. Like below-ground archaeology, it involves identifying the later developments and (mentally) removing them to reveal the original house. This archaeology always starts with a close study of the individual house, which can, of course, be very well done by its owner – but to recognise the significance of some small detail may only be possible through a wide knowledge of other houses in the region; a single peg-hole in a rafter can for instance show the location of the smoke louvre in a medieval open hall. Ordinary houses always have individual characteristics in their details and the changes they have undergone, but whether they are Regency terrace houses or medieval timber-framed halls, they share plans, structural forms and decoration with other houses of their region. Indeed, from the opposite viewpoint, this shared character is what creates the vernacular architecture of an area. Thus, the understanding of one house is complemented by comparison to others of the same type, identifying both the similarities and the individualities and, in particular, suggesting what sections may have been demolished or rebuilt. A few houses, of course, are so idiosyncratic as to be truly unique but they are exceptional.

For help with understanding village houses, the literature is extensive but the main problem is that of regional style; excellent books on medieval houses in Kent are of little help in understanding eighteenth century cottages in Lancashire. A few general studies have been published (see bibliography) but many areas have only descriptions of individual houses without much regional synthesis. Sources for understanding and dating the structure and detailing of urban houses from the seventeenth century onwards are sparse, though the books by Gray and Quiney are useful. Fortunately, documents are more likely to give dating evidence for this type of house than for those in villages.

Images

Early photographs of your house are obviously important for their general interest – they often feature the families who lived there (cf. Fig. 8.1b). They can also be particularly useful in showing alterations to the structure of the house, the addition or removal of parts, changes to windows or doors. It is therefore always valuable to search out whatever early images may be available. Photographic sources vary greatly by region but the CRO and local studies collections are good places to start. For houses of some architectural significance, the National Monuments Record in the appropriate country may be able to help (addresses in Further Reading and Resources). These houses may also have been recorded in artist's drawings or topographical prints; such images are more difficult to locate than photographs but some national indexes do exist. House plans may be found in the British Architectural Library (Royal Institute of British Architects). From the mid-nineteenth century onwards, plans for buildings in many towns had to be approved by the local council and these have often survived in large numbers in CROs. These are further discussed in Chapter 6.

---

1   As well as the volumes of the Survey of London, see, for example, Roger H. Leech, *Early industrial housing: The Trinity Area of Frome*, HMSO, 1981; Walter Ison, *The Georgian buildings of Bath from 1700 to 1830*, Kingsmead, 1980; Maurice Beresford, *East End, West End: the face of Leeds during urbanisation, 1684-1842*, Thoresby Society. Publications; v.60-61, 1988; Lyndon F Cave, *Royal Leamington Spa: its history and development*, Phillimore, 1988; Mervyn Miller, *The archive photograph series: Letchworth Garden City*, Chalford, 1995; Derek Walker, *The architecture and planning of Milton Keynes*, Architectural Press, 1982.

2   A number of regional groups exist of people interested in local building traditions, and their members can often give useful information. Most of these groups can be contacted via the Vernacular Architecture Group (see Further Reading).

3   For this technique, see M. Baillie, *A slice through time,* Batsford, 1995. During the last twenty years, tree-ring dating (dendrochronology) has revolutionised our knowledge of the development of buildings but the technique is unfortunately expensive and does not always give results. It is very important to understand the relationship of the samples dated to the development of the house and to establish that they belong to the original construction.

4   The work of Roger Leech on Bristol can be mentioned as an example: *The Topography of Medieval and Early Modern Bristol: Part I*, Bristol Record Society, Vol. 47, 1997.

5   As an example, fifteenth century deeds for the farm Voggis Hill, Sidbury, Devon are easily found in the archives of Huyshe of Sand (Devon RO 2530M), though establishing a complete sequence of owners and tenants is much more difficult. The carpentry of the house strongly suggests that the earliest deeds relate to the period when the existing house was built.

3. The Evidence of Maps

Researching the documentary history of a house will generally start by looking at historic maps, with a number of objectives. The house needs to be located in its historic parish, so that indexes can be usefully consulted;[1] the first appearance of a relatively modern house on maps gives an indication of its building date; the apportionments for tithe maps are the most accessible source for the names of owners and tenants. Maps can be divided into two groups: what may be called 'simple' maps, where the map alone provides the historical evidence, and maps associated with descriptions of the area mapped. The latter include *Tithe* and *Enclosure* maps, *Estate* maps, the *1910 Domesday* maps and the *1940-43 National Farm Survey* maps. Building plans could be considered with maps in this chapter, but their principal evidence concerns the house itself and they are therefore discussed in Chapter 6.

Generally, research will start with a simple map, such as the first large-scale Ordnance Survey edition, then look for maps with ownership information, starting with the earliest available. Finally, details will be filled in from any other maps that can be found. The 1910 Domesday maps and Field Books are particularly informative but, because a visit to the PRO is needed to look at them (as also for the National Farm Survey), they may well be deferred.

Simple Maps

All types of maps can be used to identify the first appearance of a building, giving an approximate construction date, and to follow changes in its 'footprint', the addition of wings or lean-tos or, of course, their demolition. It is therefore very valuable to identify as many maps for the area of interest as possible. For simple maps, the obvious starting points are the first editions of the large-scale Ordnance Survey maps, either at 6 in. to the mile scale (1:10560) or 25 in. (1:2500), for which national surveys were carried out between 1853 and 1888; major urban areas were surveyed at larger scale (usually 1:500) at the same time.[2] The first published editions of the 1 in. OS maps show too little detail to be much use for building history. However, the original survey drawings for the southern half of England made at 2 in. to the mile are in the British Library Map Department and give useful extra details (surveyed 1784-1841);[3] the 1 in. maps for England north of a line from Preston to Hull were based on the original 6 in. surveys. Other early printed maps are generally too schematic to identify houses.

Many towns were mapped in the 1850s under the auspices of their newly-created Boards of Health. These large-scale maps give detailed building outlines and also provide what are usually the earliest reliable mappings of tenement boundaries, which can be of great value for working out the place of a particular house in the town's sequence of development. These maps are usually in the appropriate local record office.

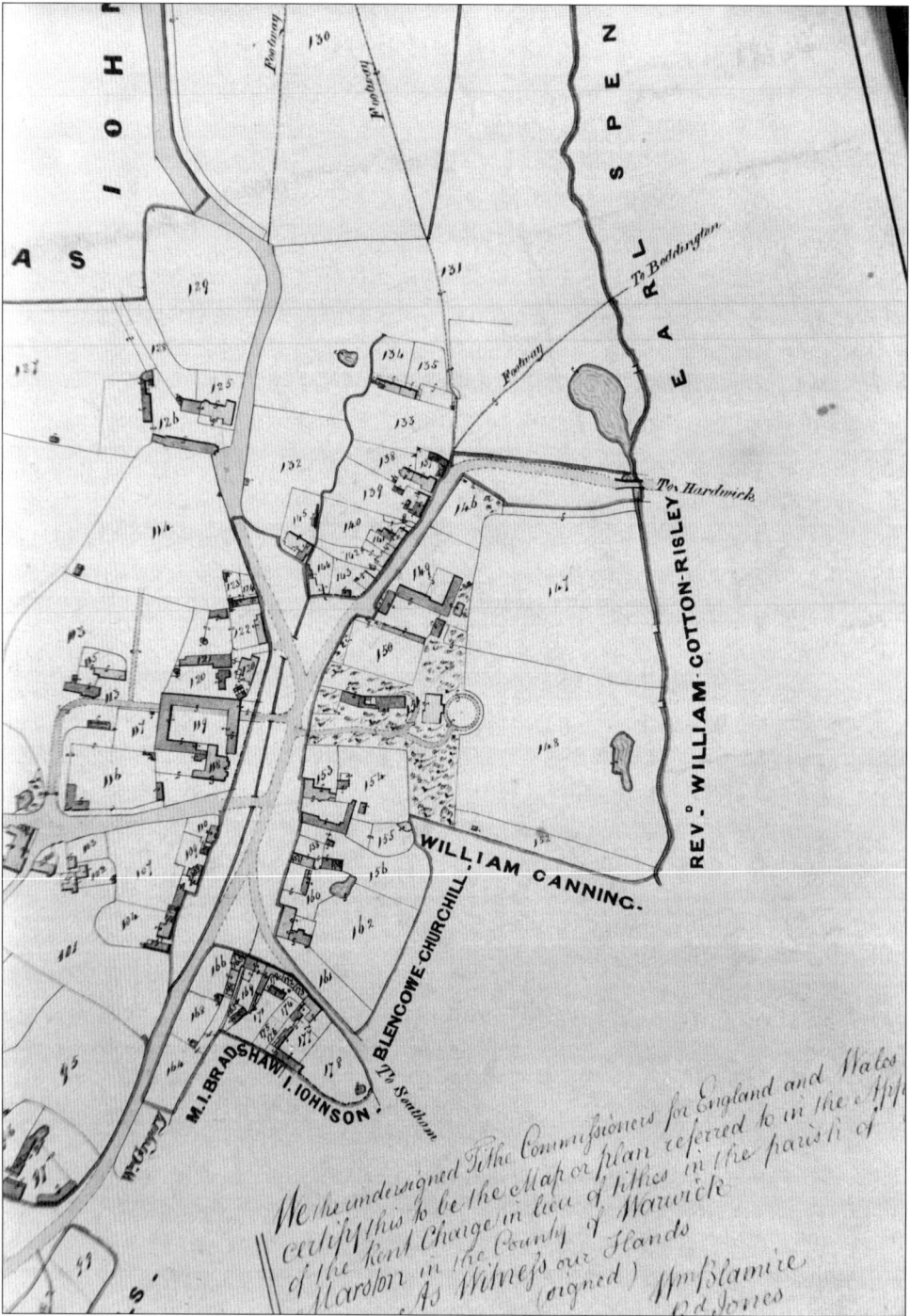

Fig. 3.1: Section of a Tithe Map for the village centre of Priors Marston, Warwickshire
(WCRO CR569/170; 1848).

Maps with additional information

Tithe Maps

The conversion of tithe payments in kind to money, following the *Tithe Redemption Act* of 1836, led in the 1840s to the large-scale mapping of about half the parishes in England and Wales; an atlas locating all these tithe maps has been published.[4] In principle, three copies of each tithe map were made. The parish copies have only rarely survived but are sometimes found among parish records in County ROs. The diocesan copies, in diocesan or county ROs, have often been very heavily used and sometimes have damaged areas. A third complete set of maps is in the PRO, derived from the Tithe Commission Office (IR30, with the apportionments in IR129); these are often in much better condition than CRO copies.[5] Although in principle the diocesan copies are identical to the PRO maps, many show differences, often in their degree of finish and sometimes in the information they give.[6]

Tithe maps and their associated apportionments are valuable to house historians in several ways. They show the footprint of each house and its associated farm buildings (the latter usually in different colours) (Fig. 3.1). The apportionments identify the fields associated with each farm, including their type of cultivation. Thus, the agricultural economy of the parish can be reconstructed from the pattern of farm sizes and cropping,[7] and the relationship of a particular house to the whole parish established – whether it was among the large farms, the small-holdings or the cottages; however, in interpreting this information you must bear in mind that circumstances change; a pair of cottages in 1845 may very often have been a farmhouse in 1650.

The information in the Tithe Apportionment for the owner and occupier of the farm is particularly important. The owner given is generally the 'beneficial owner' (who received the rents and profits), ignoring the complications of family settlements and trustees, and of types of tenure, whether freehold or copyhold.[8] The tithe maps are close enough in date to 1832, the end of the Quarter Sessions Land Tax series (p. 19), for properties to be linked from the maps back to the tax assessments; if later Land Tax records survive, linking should be even easier. The names of owners may also point the way to finding other information, such as title deeds.

Enclosure Maps

Before 1840, some property was freed from the liability to pay tithes, and thus is not included on Tithe Maps. The commonest reason for land to be tithe-free was that the parish underwent enclosure by Parliamentary Act in the eighteenth or nineteenth centuries. The reallocated lands normally included allotments to the rector and/or vicar of land in lieu of their rights to tithe, extinguishing the obligation to pay tithes and removing the need to make a tithe map.[9] Parliamentary enclosure was very common in the open-field counties of Midland England, such as Warwickshire and Leicestershire, so tithe maps are relatively rare there: only 50% of Warwickshire parishes are mapped (many incompletely) in comparison to Devon's 97%. Tithe payments due from previously enclosed small fields and house closes within villages were usually extinguished during enclosure, unless many owners did not also have open-field land. This happened in Priors Marston, Warwickshire which therefore has a magnificent tithe map covering just the village houses and closes (Fig. 3.1).[10] Undoubtedly, eighteenth century enclosure awards were always accompanied by maps, but they have rarely survived for awards dating from before about 1800; after that date the maps were usually deposited in Quarter Sessions records, accompanying the enrolled detailed award. Thus, many parishes which underwent Parliamentary enclosure in the eighteenth century have no surviving maps showing property ownership before 1910.

An important source for maps when enclosure was by private agreement is the Public Record Office. Many such agreements were strengthened by having the details recorded in Chancery decrees, with the enclosure map forming part of the record.[11] Many of these maps are listed in the published PRO catalogue, *Maps and Plans in the Public Record Office, vol. 1*. Recently discovered examples are in a card catalogue at the PRO. When an enclosure map can be located, it generally covers not only the newly enclosed land but also the old enclosures, and even cottages and closes whose owners had no interests in the open fields. It should identify owners (sometimes also tenants) and the land associated with each house as well as the footprint of the buildings and the farmyards. These maps are particularly significant because the enclosure often initiated a period of rapid social change, with the consolidation of land-holdings, the building of new farmhouses away from the village in the former open fields, and the down-grading of surplus farmhouses into cottages. For example, in Sawbridge, an east Warwickshire village enclosed in 1756, a medieval house originally associated with one yardland in the open fields (about 30 acres), had by 1800 been subdivided into six landless cottages.[12]

Reconstructing an enclosure map

When no enclosure map has survived, it is usually possible to reconstruct the layout of the enclosure allotments from the text of the award, by comparison to the later field layout and ownership evidence. Such reconstructions are almost always useful and worth the hard work involved. Even though awards rarely give details of the old enclosures in the village centre, the boundaries (abuttals) of the allotments near the village may well identify the owners of particular 'Home Closes' and therefore of the houses standing in them; such a reconstruction gave a vital clue to the former ownership of the house in Sawbridge just mentioned. Similarly, documents relating to the allotments of open-field land formerly associated with a particular farm may include evidence for the original farmhouse (see Case Study 4).

Other Tithe-free Land

Apart from land where the tithes were extinguished at enclosure, land formerly owned by monasteries was often tithe-free. In the Middle Ages, the right to the tithes from such land was often granted to the monastic owner (occasionally to a different monastery). Following the Dissolution, before the Crown disposed of the land, the tithe liability for such property was merged with the ownership. On tithe maps, such areas of monastic land are normally left blank; this is unhelpful for map-based research but gives a useful hint about sources to investigate for earlier ownership.

Estate maps, surveys and rentals

Estate maps

Estate maps, if they exist for the area being researched, are particularly valuable; they are often earlier than other detailed maps, normally dating between the late sixteenth and the mid-nineteenth centuries. For finding both estate maps and maps in sale particulars (below), the researcher usually needs to look at all the references to the parish concerned, as it is difficult to decide without looking at a map whether it covers the right area.[13]

For the components of the estate itself, a map and the survey with which it is usually associated are invaluable.[14] The map should provide all the graphical evidence found on other maps, while the written survey should list the different farms, their fields, tenants, rent, etc. Maps also sometimes give unanticipated bonuses, such as pictures of houses or cultivation details. Even when a particular house did not belong to the estate concerned, its ownership may be identified on the map and sometimes its fields and buildings are planned in outline.

One difficulty with estate maps can be the identification of particular buildings if the map was not surveyed very accurately, or if the landscape has changed considerably. Sometimes, measurements may need to be taken from a modern OS map relating the building to points that can be identified on the earlier map, such as road junctions or field boundaries. These can then be scaled and measured out on the estate map.

Estate rentals and surveys

Strictly, rentals and surveys without maps belong with documents for leasehold property in Chapter 6, but they are so closely related to estate maps that they are best be discussed here. Estate surveys give similar information to that on estate maps but are much commoner. However, unless they can be related to a map, or the house being studied has a historic name, it may be difficult to identify the relevant entry until the research is well advanced. Estate rentals give much less information than surveys, usually only listing tenant's names and their rent. However, series of rentals can be very useful in establishing the sequence of occupiers of an individual property. Even if the holding does not have a distinctive name, the succession of tenants can usually be reconstructed from the amount of rent paid and the position of the entry in each rental. To identify a particular house, it is important to start with a rental that can be correlated with a map, so that the relevant entry can be located.

Other sources of maps

Sale particulars

From about 1850, particulars for the sale of farms and estates (and of urban property) usually included maps. They show what land was associated with the house and are obviously very useful if no earlier map exists.[15] The conditions of sale may also give the 'root of title', the deed from which the seller's ownership was traced. This can be an important clue if other evidence of the house's history is difficult to find. It is usually worthwhile searching for any particulars relating to a village of interest. Even if they do not cover the particular house being studied, their maps will often name the owners of adjacent properties (see Case Study 4).

1910 'Domesday' records

The maps and valuations compiled for the Finance (1909-10) Act (often called the 'Domesday of Land') are relatively late in comparison to the other sources considered here, but they come close to giving a complete snapshot of houses and their ownership at the beginning of the twentieth century. For difficult problems, these records may well be the best available starting point and, even when other evidence abounds, they give useful background information.

Fig. 3.2: Portion of a 1910 'Domesday' map for Prior's Marston, Warwickshire. For the Field Book for hereditament 30 on this map, see Fig. 6.4 . The hereditament numbers and boundaries are marked in red on the original and are therefore clearer than on this reproduction. (PRO IR129/8/254).

The 'Domesday of Land' records are not altogether easy to use and will be discussed in some detail because of their importance.[16] They are of three main types (i) two groups of maps which identify individual properties (the *hereditaments*), mostly in the PRO (classes IR121, IR124-135), the rest in CROs, (ii) Valuation Books which summarise ownership and value (one line per property) (CROs) (iii) Field Books describing each property on four pages with 100 properties in each book (PRO IR58). The Valuation and Field Books list properties in numerical order according to their 'hereditament number'; each separately owned or occupied property has a different number. These numbers can only be worked out from the maps, except for named farms or numbered houses in town streets, when the number may be located in the Valuation Books.

The PRO holds the master series of maps, mostly 25 in. OS maps (a few at other scales). On these, each hereditament is outlined and numbered, and in the margin the 'Income Tax Parish' is named; Fig. 3.2 shows an extract from one of these maps.[17] CROs hold much less complete series of 'Working Maps' with the same information as the PRO series, sometimes with later amendments. It is always worth checking for a local map copy, to save time in identifying the hereditament number at the PRO. It is also helpful to identify in advance the 25 in. sheet number (and if necessary the 6 in. or 1:500 sheet), to avoid ordering the wrong PRO sheet.[18]

Knowing the hereditament number, the entries in the Valuation Book and the Field Book can be identified. The additional information in the Field Book is particularly relevant to building historians (see Chapter 6 and Fig. 6.4). Each entry includes a description of the house and often a sketch plan of the house or farmyard. In one respect, however, the Valuation Books are more useful than the Field Books. In the latter, subsidiary properties (such as cottages in the same ownership) are often included with the main property and they may not be fully described; the Valuation Books normally list each individual hereditament separately.

The 1910 'Domesday' records survive very extensively for England and Wales,[19] but they do have some random gaps due to accidents of survival.[20] Systematic absences relate to the property of some major landowners. It was found that the information could not be conveniently summarised in the Valuation Books and instead, files were opened, using the 'FORM 4' sheets that had been completed by the owners for their property. These files have not survived but, fortunately, these major estates are the most likely to retain their own records, sometimes even including their FORM 4 sheets.[21]

The 1940-43 National Farm Surveys

After an initial farm survey in 1940, for which few records survive, a comprehensive survey was carried out in 1941-3. It covers some 300,000 farms and small-holdings in England and Wales and includes both maps and descriptions of each farm.[22] The descriptions give the names of owners and occupiers, acreage and quality of land, crops and stock, labour and machinery, and other aspects of its management. Candid notes were made on the quality of the farm, including personal factors such as the competence of the farmer. One farmer in Priors Marston, Warwickshire was castigated as having:

No knowledge of arable cultivations – no implements – lack of co-operation
while for the farm:

Arable land lies very wet. Behind with ploughing and planting. Some pastures very wet.[23]

The survey does not describe the farmhouses in any detail, apart from basic information on water and electricity supplies, but is useful in identifying tenants and owners, as well as showing how the farm was being used.

To locate the documents, the appropriate map sheet needs to be identified (PRO class MAF73); an index volume to the class is on open shelves in the PRO. The record sheets (MAF 32) are filed by parish (identified by county sub-numbers and parish numbers) and each farm has a farm number (found from the map). Thus, Lapworth, Warwickshire is on MAF73/43/25 (Fig. 3.3) and the description of one property, Catesby Farm, is no. 42 in MAF32/961 Pt I/145 (Fig. 3.4).[24]

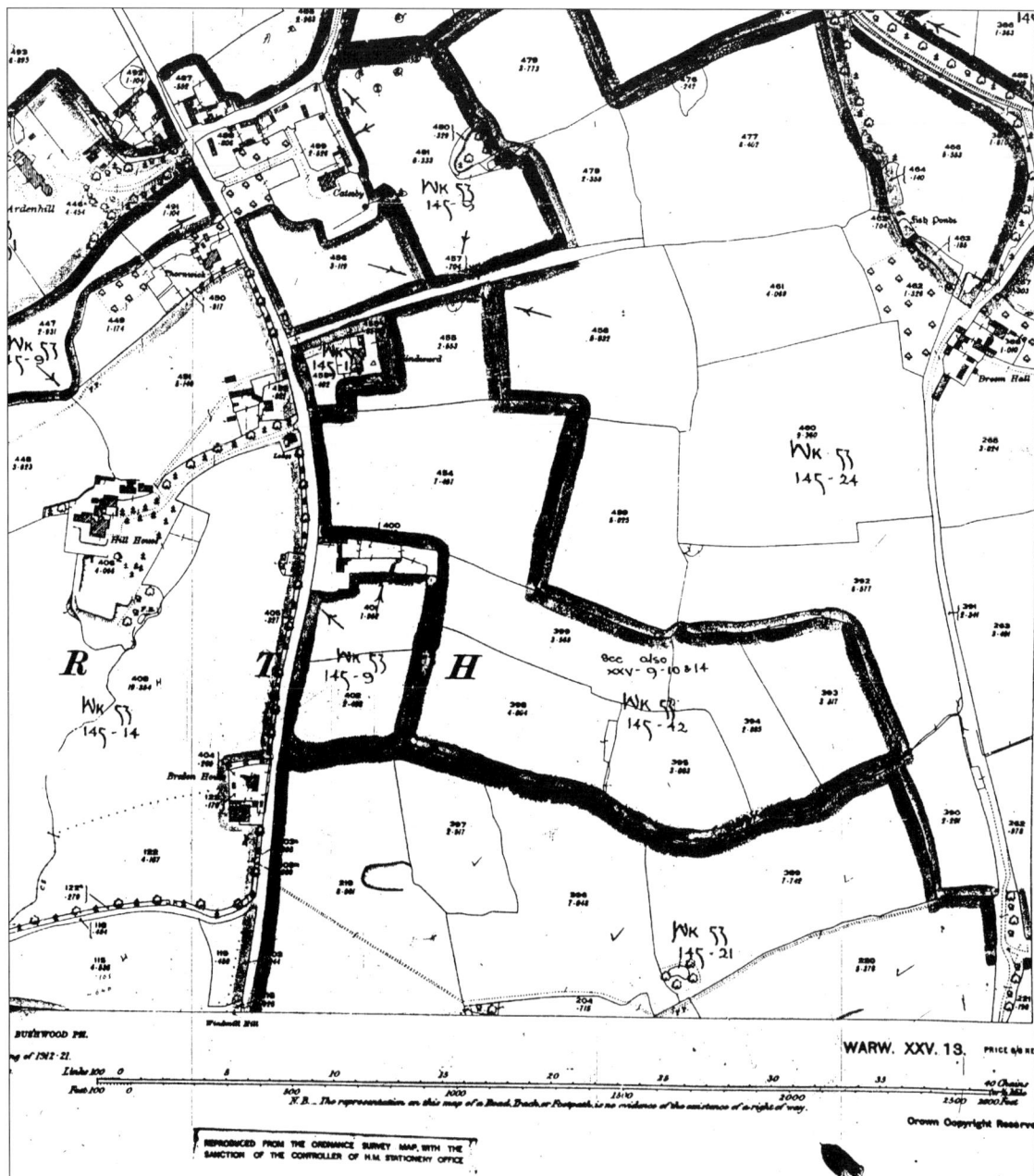

Fig. 3.3: Map of part of Lapworth, Warwickshire from the 1941-3 National Farm Survey. Catesby Farm is WK53 145-42 (PRO MAF73/43/25).

FARM SURVEY

County _Warwickshire_   Code No. _WW/53   145/42   D19/42_

District _D - Leamington_   Parish _Lapworth_

Name of holding _CATESBY FARM_   Name of farmer _ARMSTRONG. R.S._

Address of farmer _UPLANDS FARM, LAPWORTH, WARWICK_

Number and edition of 6-inch Ordnance Survey Sheet containing farmstead _25 SW 1925_

A. TENURE.

1. Is occupier tenant   ...   .
   owner   ...   .   ✗
2. If tenant, name and address of owner :—
   1) _Capt Dammers_
      Catesby Farm, Lapworth
   2) _M.s.s Johnson, Windward, Lapworth_
      _(O.S 454, 455)_

3. Is farmer full time farmer   ...   .   ✗
   part time farmer   ...   ...
   spare time farmer   ...
   hobby farmer   ...   ...
   other type   ...   ...
   Other occupation, if any :—

		Yes	No
4. Does farmer occupy other land ?			✗

Name of Holding	County	Parish
✓ _Upland Fm_	_Warwicks_	_Lapworth_
1/114 _Pear Tree Fm_	"	_Balsall_

		Yes	No
5. Has farmer grazing rights over land not occupied by him ?			✗

If so, nature of such rights—

B. CONDITIONS OF FARM.

1. Proportion (%) of area on which soil is	Heavy	Medium	Light	Peaty
		_100_		

2. Is farm conveniently laid out ?   Yes ...   ...
   Moderately   ✗
   No ...   ...

3. Proportion (%) of farm which is	Good	Fair	Bad
naturally	_100_		
4. Situation in regard to road ...		✗	
5. Situation in regard to railway ...	✗		
6. Condition of farmhouse	–	–	–
Condition of buildings	–	–	–
7. Condition of farm roads	–	–	–
8. Condition of fences	✗		
9. Condition of ditches	✗		
10. General condition of field drainage		✗	
11. Condition of cottages	–	–	–

		No.
12. Number of cottages within farm area ...		_N_
Number of cottages elsewhere		_1_
13. Number of cottages let on service tenancy ...		_L_

14. Is there infestation with :—	Yes	No
rabbits and moles		✗
rats and mice		✗
rooks and wood pigeons ...		✗
other birds		✗
insect pests		✗
15. Is there heavy infestation with weeds ?		✗

If so, kinds of weeds :—

	Yes	No
16. Are there derelict fields ?		✗

If so, acreage ... ...

FORM No. B496/E.I.

C. WATER AND ELECTRICITY.

	Pipe	Well	Roof	Stream	None
Water supply :—					
1. To farmhouse ...	–	–	–	–	–
2. To farm buildings ...	–	–	–	–	–
3. To fields					

	Yes	No
4. Is there a seasonal shortage of water ?...		✗
Electricity supply :—		
5. Public light		✗
Public power		✗
Private light		✗
Private power		✗
6. Is it used for household purposes ? ...		✗
Is it used for farm purposes ?		✗

D. MANAGEMENT.

1. Is farm classified as A, B or C ?   ...   ... _B+_

2. Reasons for B or C :—					
old age		
lack of capital		
personal failings		

If personal failings, details :—

	Good	Fair	Poor	Bad
3. Condition of arable land ...		✗		
4. Condition of pasture ...		✗		

	Adequate	To some extent	Not at all
5. Use of fertilisers on :—			
arable land ...	✗		
grass land ...	✗		

Field information recorded by

Lo. J. Hollick

Date of recording _8.4.42_

This primary record completed by

Neate

Date _29.11.43_

*15946. Wt.46166/817. 3000 pads. 3/41. Wy.L.P. Gp.676.

Fig. 3.4: 1941-3 National Farm Survey, entry for Catesby Farm, Lapworth, Warwickshire (PRO MAF 32/961 Pt.I/145, item 42)

Difficult Cases

Sometimes only OS maps can be discovered but not maps keyed to ownership. In this case, the area of the property has to be established from title deeds or other sources, while owners and tenants will need to be traced using the sources discussed in the next chapter. With such problems, it is more important than otherwise to examine groups of properties – all the houses in the village street, for example, as other houses may provide information not available for the primary object of the research.

---

1   For identifying some earlier documents, the *Hundred* will also be useful (the sub-county administrative units preceding districts and rural districts); they can be identified from the *Victoria County History*, the *Place Names of England* (both if published for the area), or county histories; the County RO can also be expected to provide this information.

2   Richard Oliver, *O. S. Maps: a concise guide for historians*, Charles Close Society, 1993.

3   British Library: MAPS O.S.D. + sheet number. They have been reproduced on microfiche by the British Library and copies are held by some ROs.

4   R J P Kain & R P Oliver, *The Tithe Maps of England and Wales*, Cambridge University Press, 1995; see also R Kain and S Wilmot, 'Tithe surveys in national and local archives', *Archives*, 20 (1992), 106-117. It should be noted that not all the maps cover the whole of their parish in detail. In some parishes, especially in the Midlands, only the small areas with un-redeemed tithes are mapped.

5   Most are now produced as microfiche copies, which are easy to use but have problems in establishing their scale and sometimes in their legibility.

6   See R Kain and S Wilmot, 'Tithe surveys in national and local archives', *Archives*, 20 (1992), 106-117.

7   Other sources, of course, contribute evidence of the agricultural economy. See the *Guides to Local History* in Further Reading.

8   Three-life leasehold (see p. 30) had generally disappeared by the 1840s.

9   Quite often, some land remained liable to tithes, e.g. unenclosed heaths, so a map was later produced but this only covers a small part of the parish in detail.

10 WCRO CR569/170.

11 The maps have generally been transferred to the artificial classes MPA to MPZ (mainly MPA and MPB for maps from Chancery and Exchequer documents), but the class lists include references to the original documents.

12 N W Alcock and C T Paul Woodfield, 'Social pretensions in architecture and ancestry: Hall House, Sawbridge, Warwickshire and the Andrewe family', *Antiquaries Journal*, **76** (1996), 51-72.

13 Warwickshire CRO has a series of key maps (compiled by a researcher) on which the coverage of all known estate maps for the county (whether in the RO or not) have been marked. This is an exceptionally valuable resource that can be commended to other ROs or their volunteers.

14 For small properties, the survey details are frequently written on the map itself.

15 The lots in which an estate was divided for sale may not correspond to its former tenancies, but the names of the tenants as listed in the sale particulars should show this.

16 For full details of the documents and their context, see B. Short, *Land and society in Edwardian Britain*, Cambridge University Press, 1997.

17 The Field Books are organised by Income Tax Parish, so it is necessary to identify this from the Record Map, the Valuation Book or an index volume at the PRO (shelved with the lists for IR121, 124-135).

18 Identifying the specific call number from the on-line catalogue (PROCAT) is difficult in the current version of the catalogue as individual entries do not include the name of the county. Thus, you need to search for the sheet (e.g. XIII 13 for a 25in. sheet or XXXIII 7 13 for a 1:500 sheet) but only in the particular class(es) within IR124-135 that relates to the appropriate county (or IR121 for London).

19 For Scotland and Ireland, consult the corresponding Public Record Offices.

20   Much of the material for Hampshire was lost in the Second World War and in Warwickshire, the PRO has no maps for Coventry though it does hold the Field Books, while the Working Maps and Valuation Books are in Coventry RO. For the parish of Knowle, Warwickshire, the PRO has no records at all; Warwickshire CRO has map sheets but the Valuation Book is missing; it does have an incomplete series of the records known as 'FORM 37', which are copies of the Valuation Book entries as sent out to landowners.

21   For example, those for the 100 London properties of the Pell family are in Cambridge University Library, Doc. 4002. It is not clear how many major estates were treated in this way, nor whether dummy Field Book entries were compiled for their property.

22   The National Archives of Scotland holds similar maps for Scotland, but the descriptions have not survived.

23   PRO MAF32/963 Pt.I/219 no. 11.

24   For further information on the survey, see PRO leaflet 106, *National Farm Surveys of England and Wales, 1940-1943* and Nick Barratt, *Tracing the history of your house*, Public Record Office, 2001, p. 31f.

No. 2.

LAND TAX ASSESSMENT, 1826.

In the Parish of *Lapworth*

in the Division of *Kington*

in the County of *Warwick*

An Assessment made for granting an Aid to His Majesty by a LAND TAX, to be raised in *Great Britain*, for the Service of the Year One Thousand Eight Hundred and Twenty-six, in Pursuance of an Act passed in the Thirty-eighth Year of the Reign of His late Majesty Geo. III. intituled "An Act for granting an Aid to His Majesty by a "LAND TAX, to be raised in *Great Britain*, for the Service of the Year One "Thousand Seven Hundred and Ninety Eight," and of another Act passed in the Forty-second of His said late Majesty's Reign intituled, "An Act for consolidating ' the Provisions of the several Acts passed for the Redemption and Sale of the Land "Tax into One Act, and for making further Provision for the Redemption and Sale "thereof."

Assessed by Us

Joseph Osborn
John Mortiboyes } ASSESSORS.

We do hereby return
John Mortiboyes
limits and bounds of the said Parish of
to be Collectors of the Monies as aforesaid.

Joseph Osborn —— and
as able and sufficient Persons, living within the
Lapworth in the County of Warwick.
Joseph Osborn
John Mortiboyes } ASSESSORS.

Rentals.	Names of Proprietors.	Names of Occupiers.	Names or Description of Estates or Property.	Sums Assessed and Exonerated.			Sums Assessed and not Exonerated.		
				£	s	d	£	s	d
	John Burman Gent	Anchor Thos	House and Land	"	"	"	1	14	0
	The Executors of the late Thos Fetherston Esqr	Ball Saml	Do	"	"	"	3	3	2
	Benjn Bissell	Bissell Benjn	Do	"	"	"	4	1	4
	Martha Lea	Billings Jonathan	Do	"	"	"	1	18	5¼
	John Brook	Canning Saml	Do	"	"	"	2	17	0
	Revd K. N.Nye	Child Revd and Co	Do	9	6	0	1	12	0
	John Burman Gent	Cox Will	Do	"	"	"	2	0	0
	Benjn Hilduk	Chinn John	Do	"	"	"	1	2	6
	Saml Cramnor	Cramnor Saml	Do	"	"	"	1	0	0
	Charles Fetherston Esqr	Fetherston & Wakefield	Land	"	"	"	2	13	10
	Do	Fellows Jos	House and Land	"	"	"	3	6	4
	Do	Fetherston Charles Esq	Do	1	12	4	"	"	"
	Isaac Green	Green Isaac	Do	"	"	"	"	15	11¼
	Jos Hobday	Green John	House and Garden	"	3	0¼	"	"	"
	Willm Ingram Gent	Hands George	House and Land	16	13	0	"	"	"
	Benjn Hildick	Hildick Moses	Do	"	"	"	3	5	5
	Revd John Ellis	Haynes George	Do	"	"	"	1	2	4
	Saml Allen	Hickin Charles	Do	2	10	0	"	"	"
	Lord Cornwallis	Hill Ann	Do	4	16	0	"	"	"
	Do	Hill Ann	Do	4	17	0	"	"	"
	Do	Hill Henry	Do	0	13	4	"	"	"
	Sir Charles Cockerill	Hodges George &c	Do	43	11	11	"	"	"
	Thos Johns	Johns Thos	Do	"	"	"	3	3	0
	Do	Johns Thos	Do	"	"	"	1	12	0
	Thos Burman Gent	Burman Thos	Do	2	7	0	"	"	"
				94	10	11¼	36	19	1½

Fig. 4.1: Part of a Land Tax assessment, for Lapworth, Warwickshire in 1826. Note the distinction between exonerated and not exonerated sums (WCRO, QS11/7/49)

4. The succession of owners and tenants

Once the house has been found on as many maps as possible and the owners and occupiers identified at one or more dates, the next task is to establish the succession of earlier and later owners. Sources of evidence for such sequences are very varied and differ considerably from place to place and even from house to house, so what follows is not a comprehensive guide. The most widely available material comes from the Land Tax assessments, but other sources include rate books, and directories. Generally, any information that links owners or occupiers to some payment or responsibility can be useful. Thus in some villages the requirement to repair given lengths of the churchyard wall was associated with particular properties and lists of those responsible ('Panel Lists') can be used to correlate ownership.[1]

Land Tax Assessments

The Land Tax Assessments are one of the most valuable systematic sources for owners and tenants, because they exist for almost every parish for the late eighteenth to early nineteenth centuries; they can therefore be used to carry back the information from the 1840s Tithe Maps for 50 or 60 years. The grant of a national tax on land was first made in 1692, but the assessments survive systematically among Quarter Sessions records for almost all counties only from about 1780 to 1832; they were preserved because of their evidence for entitlement to vote (Fig. 4.1). The tax was only abolished in 1963, and the later assessments are, if anything, even more useful as they can be linked with census listings and the 1909-10 Valuation Act sources, but they rarely survive. Assessments from before 1780 have occasionally been preserved (generally in parish collections) and are very useful for this period, when other sequence evidence is sparse.[2]

The annual assessments list all occupiers of land (apart occasionally from cottagers) with the amount assessed and, from about 1790, they also include the owners and the nature of the property (house and land, or land alone).[3] Thus, by following names through from year to year, sequences of owners and occupiers can be established. For parishes with a Tithe Map, it is usually possible to correlate the 1840s owners and occupiers with those in the 1832 Land Tax and so form a sequence back to 1780. Without a Tithe Map, some other starting point is needed, which might be another early map, the farm name (if it is included in the Land Tax list), the occupier's name in a directory or a deed. For difficult cases, it might be necessary to identify the entry in the Land Tax by examining all the alternatives.

Land Tax assessment values

Some technical aspects of the Land Tax need to be considered. The total assessment for each parish was fixed in 1698 and remained unchanged throughout the life of the tax, though the poundage (rate charged per £1 of valuation) varies; from 1780, it was charged at 4s in the £1. Similarly, within each parish the assessments for each property were generally constant, originating perhaps in the values used for a church or poor rate when the tax was first imposed. Only in 1878, were the assessments recalculated in relation to the notional or actual rental value of each property. Thereafter, the tax on an individual property could vary year-by-year, as the total rental value for the parish changed but the total assessment did not. At this period, also, the number of properties taxed might be increased by including cottages previously passed over.[4] From 1796 onwards, landowners were able to 'exonerate' their Land Tax liability by payment of a lump sum. These exonerated assessments are generally still included in the lists, but there can have been little incentive to keep the names of tenants precisely up-to-date, so they need to be used with caution.

The Land Tax values have been used to estimate property values or relative wealth,[5] but the results have been found to be unreliable. Presumably when the assessments were originally set up in 1698, they did reflect relative values within a parish fairly well, but as they were not updated, they ignore such changes as improvement of a property. Comparison of values between different parishes are particularly suspect. However, the overall economic structure of a parish is revealed by the number of properties listed and the spread of their assessments. The position of a particular property in the economic hierarchy can then be determined. In principle, the 1798 national series of assessments can also be used for regional comparisons.

Rate Assessments

Householders in each parish (sometimes property owners rather than occupiers) were responsible for paying for repairs to the church (administered by the churchwardens), for the highways (highway overseers) and, especially, for poor relief (overseers of the poor and later the Poor Law Unions); in a few places, rates were levied for drainage or sea-wall repairs. Each of these liabilities was collected through the same type of assessment as the Land Tax. Each property had a value associated with it and the assessment was made at a certain rate, say 2d in the pound. Rural parishes did sometimes revise their valuations but generally these remained fixed until the later nineteenth century. However, towns often levied rates according to the rent of a property, making adjustments whenever this changed. In principle, all these rates should have produced annual or more frequent assessments, but in reality the account books often say 'from a 1d rate, £3', without itemising the individual payments, and few assessments are preserved for rural parishes. When they do survive, they can be correlated with the Land Tax lists and used to extend ownership sequences.

In larger towns, poor rates have a much better chance of surviving; thus, for Birmingham they exist from 1736 onwards. Tracing properties by the amount of their assessment is more difficult than for rural property because of the changing valuations, but the rate lists are generally set out in a standard order, normally going up one side of a street and down the other. Early rate books often do not give the street, let alone the house number, so identifying particular properties can be very difficult. However, the lists of properties in the rate books can be correlated with deed evidence, directories or other listings, or extended into a period when street numbers were used – or even to 1910 if no earlier sources exist. Just as the Land Tax assessments can be followed back from the Tithe Map, so one generally starts with a late volume of the rate books, which gives street numbers or can be linked to the 1910 'Domesday' ownership, and works backward in time.[6]

As well as identifying the sequence of tenants (and owners when given), they are very useful in pin-pointing building dates for new houses and new streets. In research on a house in Acock's Green, a suburb of Birmingham, the rate books showed that a new street, Westfield Road, was laid out in 1891, though initially the relatively large properties were only described as 'land and sheds', and it took another eight years before they were subdivided and sold off for building.

Directories

For certain types of property, directories are very useful in building up the sequence of occupiers. Nationally, Kelly's Directories and their predecessors exist from around 1850 for almost all communities, but many larger towns have much earlier directories. From the mid-nineteenth century, they often give street-by-street sequences of occupiers and it may be relatively easy to identify particular houses. In villages, the directories normally list separately the principal 'private' and 'commercial' residents but they do not always give house or farm names; they include tradesmen and craftsmen but not normally cottages and their tenants. Thus, they are most useful in supplementing sources such as Land Tax assessments or poor rates, in confirming who lived where, but can be unreliable as the primary evidence for the succession of occupiers.

Other sequence evidence

Electoral registers

In 1918, the right to vote was extended to all males over 21 (women over 30); thereafter, electoral registers were compiled annually and they give full names of electors with their addresses. The registers are normally arranged by street (though sometimes alphabetically in rural parishes), so it is fairly easy to compile a sequence of the names of those living in a particular house. Before 1918, electors had to own or occupy property of a specified value (varying with time), or might be freeholders in a borough. Registers are normally arranged by voter's surname and, although they give the location of the property entitling the elector to vote, identifying those living in a particular house may well be difficult. Before 1832, electoral registers were not compiled but poll books were often printed, listing how people had voted. As well as the franchise being much more limited, poll books give even less information that might be useful to identify who lived where.[7]

Estate rentals

Estate rentals and surveys can be expected for property which belonged to a large estate. They may also be informative for freehold houses especially in boroughs, which often paid a chief rent to the lord of the manor, even if the estate did not own the house. Thus, it is worth looking at manorial rentals and other estate documents in case they give useful sequence information. For one generally very well documented parish with an almost complete series of rentals, I was able to trace property in a period for which they were missing by using the lists of suitors to the manor court (see Case Study 5; Fig. 8.13). These were not topographical in their arrangement (beyond identifying the hamlets in which people lived), but were prepared each year by crossing out those who had died or left and writing in their successors; their chief drawback was that if someone moved house, this might not be identified in the lists. These sources are discussed further in Chapter 5 under Leasehold Property.

Hearth Tax assessments

The Hearth Tax was levied from 1662 to 1688, charged at the rate of 1s per hearth every half year, with exemptions for poor people, but assessments normally only survive for the period 1662 to 1674 (with great variation from county to county).[8] The assessments are mainly of significance in showing the overall pattern of prosperity and housing standards in a parish, and in identifying the numbers of hearths in individual houses (Chapter 6). When a series of assessments survive, they can be correlated with each other to build up the succession of occupiers, but the relatively short date range means that they are of limited use for this purpose. Identifying a particular property can be difficult without a good sequence of occupiers from other evidence. However, the names are often listed in topographical sequence (perhaps up one side of the village street and down the other) so, if some properties can be identified, others may be located tentatively.

Problems

If no sequence evidence can be found and for periods when it breaks down, the main source of information will probably be title deeds (Chapter 5) and it will be necessary to build up the succession of owners and occupiers from this information; in this situation, tenants in occupation for fairly short periods may not be recorded. Thus, for one farm, title deeds gave the tenants in 1630 and 1677 as Anthony Gibbs (father and son). Probate records for both of them existed, for 1668 and 1681 respectively. However, a probate inventory of 1670 for a William Gibbs was almost word-for-word identical to that of Anthony Gibbs in 1668, so he was undoubtedly also a tenant of the farm.[9]

Sometimes it is possible to jump over a problem period and pick up the sequence at an earlier date, perhaps from an early map, the name of a farm, or from topographical records. In the small town of Henley-in-Arden, whose historic core consists of one long street, the owners of one house could be traced back to 1730 but no further. The Hearth Tax assessments were taken topographically, so, with some people located from title deeds, others can be fitted in from their positions in the lists.

---

1   The 'panels about the churchyard' and similar phrases were the contemporary descriptions of these documents in West Sussex, though they were also sometimes called 'church marks', suggesting that the sections of the wall or fence was marked to indicate who was responsible for that part. See Annabelle Hughes, 'Two Sussex examples of the contribution documentary sources can make to the study of buildings', *Vernacular Architecture*, 32 (2001), 48-53; see also Case Study 4.

2   See Jeremy Gibson, M Medlycott and Dennis Mill (eds), *Land and Window Tax assessments 1690-1950*, Federation of Family History Societies, 1997. The Quarter Sessions series have been lost for Berkshire, Cornwall, Rutland, Shropshire and Welsh counties. The assessments for a single year, 1798, are preserved nationally (PRO IR23). In the absence of local assessments, this series is valuable for showing the pattern of land ownership and occupancy, but it does not help establish a sequence of owners. Some post-1832 assessments survive for about half the counties, but none have complete series.

3   Tax was levied also on tenants of tithes and on some salaries, so these appear occasionally.

4   E. g. in the hamlet of Wilmcote in Aston Cantlow, Warwickshire in 1887, the number of properties taxed increased from 17 to 28. It was not possible to link these added entries to those in earlier assessments, but they could be followed through to the 1910 Valuation lists.

5   See M Turner & D Mills (eds) *Land and Property: The English Land Tax, 1692-1832*, Alan Sutton, 1986.

6   Of course, if the property can be identified at an earlier date (say from a Tithe Map), one can work
     both backwards and forwards from this date. It is worth bearing in mind that a particular rate book
     may include notes correlating its data with the preceding volume that will only make sense when
     working forward in time.

7   See J Gibson and C Rogers, *Electoral Registers since 1832 and Burgess Rolls*, Federation of
     Family History Societies, 1990.; J Gibson and C Rogers, *Poll Books c. 1696-1872: a directory to
     holdings in Great Britain*, Federation of Family History Societies, 1994.

8   The survival and location of Hearth Tax assessments is given in Jeremy Gibson, *Hearth Tax
     Returns and other later Stuart Tax Lists and the Association Oath Rolls*, Federation of Family
     History Societies, 1996.

9   Worcester CRO Probate Records: 1669/291 (inventory dated 18th December 1668); 1670/338;
     1681/197 (Aston Cantlow, Warwickshire). William Gibbs is not named in deeds and leases relating
     to the farm, but was probably the son of the first and brother of the second Anthony.

5. The Evidence of Deeds and Individual Documents

This chapter's primary concern is with documents that refer specifically to the house being researched, such as title deeds and leases. These are usually the best documents to give direct evidence about the house, its owners and occupiers. However, using them requires that they be discovered, which may prove difficult. The search strategy depends on the type of property being studied and this is the first aspect considered, followed by an examination of how they are interpreted.

Finding Title Deeds

Although the initial source of evidence for the history of a house will probably come from maps (Chapter 3), the beginning of the research should also see the start of what may be a long search for title deeds. It is rare that the recent history indicates that deeds will probably not be useful – this might be the case for a house that belonged to a major estate, when the place to begin is with the records of the estate. Certain special types of houses, including rectories and vicarages, former schools, toll houses and railway stations, will also generally not have very significant title deeds, but other useful records may exist.

Finding deed evidence will normally start with the modern deeds (unless old ones are already known), but the search for earlier information will be different for freehold, leasehold and copyhold property, as discussed in the following sections. Copyhold property is generally the easiest to trace, followed by leasehold, while freehold deeds are often the most difficult both to find and to interpret. It is worth remembering, though, that property often changed its character, from copyhold to freehold (Cf. Case Study 2), from freehold to leasehold, etc.

The current title deeds for a house will rarely tell the complete story from its building to the present day, but they are an essential place to start. If not in the owner's actual possession, they can usually be consulted by arrangement with the solicitor, bank or building society that holds them. The most serious problem with finding useful evidence has been the advent of compulsory registration at the Land Registry, after which the old deeds are legally superseded. Conservative solicitors may retain them with the registration document, but building societies try to dispose of them, to reduce storage needs. They may be kept by the owner's solicitor, passed back to the owner (sometimes a former owner) or thrown away; only rarely have they been passed on to the local RO, the only satisfactory long-term solution, ensuring their accessibility for the future. The result is too often the disappearance of a century or more of detailed history which can be very difficult to recover from other sources. If the current deeds start with the Land Registry Certificate, you need to enquire of your solicitor, the previous owner, or his solicitor and hope that one or other will have the earlier deeds.[1]

Sometimes, the recent deeds are inaccessible for other reasons; for a leasehold house or flat the freeholder will hold them, while if a farmhouse has been sold off from its land, they are likely to remain with the farm. In these situations, the deeds may be particularly useful in telling the story of the house, taking the story back from the time when it was separated from the rest of the property. Both the circumstances and the deeds themselves may suggest where to look next, as the following examples show. For a semi-detached house in a Birmingham suburb, the original deeds (retrieved from the solicitor) went back to 1922. An abstract of title with them showed that, when the house was built in 1899, it was owned jointly with the adjoining house; the latter's deeds filled in the first 20 years but still left the development of the site rather obscure. In fact, two pairs of houses had been built by the same developer, so that the deeds for one of the other two houses (which were not located) might extend the story further.

In the case of a small Welsh farmhouse, sold off in 1967 when a new house was built, its deeds began at that date and the abstract of title only started in 1945. The farmer allowed access to his deeds, which in fact went back no further, but he did have the abstract which preceded the 1945 sale. It showed that the sale followed the winding up of a family trust set up by a will of 1875 and, crucially, it gave the name of the Brecon solicitors who had produced the 1875 will for inspection. This firm kindly checked their records and located the deed bundle for the family trust, which started with a deed of 1786, reciting one of 1759. These showed that the farm had belonged to a family called Price for this entire period. With this clue, the family could be recognised in Theophilus Jones's nineteenth century County History for Breconshire which stated that they had possessed this and another farm since the time of Queen Elizabeth – and that another solicitor had lost the earlier title deeds in 1760!

Such direct links do not usually lead to deed evidence covering the whole period of interest for a house. Often the only way to find further evidence is by a systematic search for deeds in ROs. It is surprising how often solicitor's or estate collections will produce relevant information. They may not include the actual deed bundle for the property but deeds for one house may mention the owner of the adjoining one, or it may have been included in a marriage settlement or in a multi-property 'deed to lead the uses of a fine'.[2] The significance of such a stray will only become clear when the sequence of owners is known. Although possible sources can be located early in the research, their potential can only be realised with the help of this background knowledge. It may even prove necessary to use all the available documents to create a summary of property ownership for the whole of a village, so that the key information can be identified within this framework. This approach is very powerful, but only realistic for relatively small settlements, villages rather than towns.

Sometimes none of the deed evidence is helpful or, frustratingly, it looks as if it would be useful if only a linkage could be confirmed. Additional evidence can be sometimes be found in another source, the wills of people from the community.[3] Their preservation in diocesan archives is independent of the survival of title deeds, though it does, of course, depend on a will being made; in this context, an intestate probate administration is of little use. Property may well be described in detail in a will, not uncommonly including details of its acquisition, as well as its bequest (cf. Case Study 4). Of course, not everyone's real estate was in the village where they lived, so the wills of people from nearby, who seem likely to be owners can also be useful. Deeds also regularly mention inheritance from a previous owner, pointing the direction for further research.

Deed Registries

For two favoured areas in England, Yorkshire and Middlesex, and for Ireland, the establishment of Registries of Deeds in the early eighteenth century means that locating deeds from then onwards should be straightforward, because the evidence will exist in the registry volumes; these contain 'memorials' (i.e. abstracts) of the original deeds. Although this is true in principle, in practice it may be very difficult because of the poor quality of the indexes to the registered deeds; only the relatively small East Riding Registry has an adequate place index. Thus, though excellent evidence certainly exists, finding it can be very hard work. Case Study 3 explains how the original building lease for a house built in the 1850s in the London suburb of Hackney was located in the Middlesex Registry, hidden among hundreds of others. This one document established the date, the estate which developed the site, the builder and the first owner. Use of the Middlesex Deed Registry diminished rapidly after 1899 and it was finally closed in 1938.

The Land Registry

The national Land Registry for England and Wales was established as early as 1862; Scotland and Northern Ireland have similar but separate registries. However, the Registry was largely ignored until registration became compulsory, a process that has gradually been extended until the whole of England and Wales were included in 1990 (2003 in Northern Ireland). Thus, for many properties, the Land Registry only contains relatively modern information which is more easily available from other sources.[4] The principal exception is London, where compulsory registration was initiated in 1899 within the new County of London, so for London houses the register now covers more than a century of history. It is easy to obtain a copy of the register, for a modest fee,[5] but the results may be disappointing. The register itself only gives the date of original registration and the name and date of registration of the current owner, with information on the existence of charges, leases, etc. and, if relevant, details of covenants and conditions.

When a property is first registered, the previous title deeds are inspected to establish the owner, etc., but the deeds are then returned to the owner. However, the Registry retains copies of earlier deeds that include specific information that is still valid (e.g. restrictive covenants), which will be 'referred to' in the Register. They also hold the original deeds relating to all post-registration transactions.[6] At the time of writing, they will only provide copies of the deeds 'referred to' in the register, but a change is due to take place in October 2003, with the implementation of the Land Registration Act 2002. Thereafter, in principle the Registry will provide copies of any document they hold 'relating to an application' (including of course deeds), subject to certain exemptions; how this will work in practice has still to be decided. From October 2003, the Registrar will also provide *Historical Information* held by the Land Registry in the form of the edition of the register on a specified date, but only if it is held electronically. As the register first began to be computerised in 1986, this provision may be of relatively little use to present-day historians.

Case Study 3 (Chapter 8) includes an example information obtained from the Land Registry (before the 2003 change in the rules).

Table 5.1. Clauses in post-medieval deeds.

Adapted from N. W. Alcock, *Old Title Deeds*, Phillimore, 2001, p. 56. The phrases are usually more repetitive than shown here, e.g. an Action clause might read 'hath, granted, bargained, sold, released, and confirmed, and doth grant, bargain, sell, release and confirm'.

Clause	Text	Comments and Significance
Introduction	**This Indenture** tripartite	Bipartite (2), quadripartite, etc., depending on the number of parties
Date	**dated the**	
Parties	**Between ... of the first part and ... of the second part,** etc.	The people concerned. One party may consist of several people
	Witnesseth that	
Recital	**Whereas ...**	Describes previous transactions, sometimes very numerous
	Now the said ...	'Now' ends the recital
Consideration	**for and in consideration of ...**	Often the actual sum of money; sometimes a cautious 'for good and sufficient consideration', or 'for natural love and affection'; 5s. for minor parties. 'The end of the recital may explain how the consideration was to be paid.
Action	**doth demise** (lease) or **grant** or **release** or **assign ... unto ...**	These are the main alternatives though each is wrapped up in many more words
Property	**All that messuage ... together with all ways watercourses, ...**	The property involved. Such inclusive clauses do not mean that the property included any watercourses, etc., but guard against any omissions
	(and also ...)	Another property, or something like a right of way
	together with all title deeds ...	Alternatively 'such deeds as relate solely' to the property
	To have and to hold the said messuage ... to the said ... his heirs and assigns ...	
Period	**For the term of ...** (or) **For ever**	Distinguishes between a permanent grant and one for a limited period, long or short
Tenure	**To be holden of the chief lord ...**	Not always included. A medieval survival that can be ignored
Rent	**Yielding and paying ...**	The rent, if any
Uses	**to the use of the said ...**	Who benefits – this clause can be very complex
Conditions and Covenants	**Subject to ... and the said ... further covenanteth ...**	By far the most variable clause with both formal and significant covenants
Warranty	**And the said . . . warranteth that he hath not done any action ...**	A restatement of the right of the seller to the property
Witness	**In witness whereof the said ... hath hereunto set his name and seal the day and year above written**	
Back surface (dorse) and endorsements		Carries the witnesses to the signing, sometimes with receipts and additional memoranda, sometimes including the texts of complete deeds A summary is often written (endorsed), on the surface exposed when the deed is folded up.

THE EVIDENCE OF TITLE DEEDS

Freehold property

In studying a bundle of title deeds, it is easy to become bogged down in the legal details of each document. However, title deeds of the seventeenth to nineteenth centuries have very standard structures, so that it is possible to identify the key sections without struggling through the whole of what may be a very long document.[7] Table 5.1 gives a summary of the clauses likely to be found in such deeds which should help identify the most useful sections, the *ownership* (and how it changes) and the *description of the property*. If the deed bundle includes an Abstract of Title, this can also provide a very useful summary. More detailed understanding of the technicalities of deeds can be found with the help of the works listed under Further Reading.

Property descriptions

Occasionally, deeds mention a 'new-built' house but, as evidence for the building date, this needs to be regarded with caution; the term could be retained for a century or more. Sometimes the description is more specific as for example in a Warwickshire deed of 1792:

> All those two new erected messuages [*houses*] ... erected and built by the said Thomas Morteboys on the ground where a messuage or tenement heretofore stood ... and all other tenements devised by William Morteboys to the said Thomas Morteboys, deceased.

This clue led to the will of William Morteboys in the PRO, which was proved in 1734; Thomas died in 1779, so the house must have been built between these dates, probably in fact near the beginning of the period. The 1792 deed was the only early one found for the house and it is a typical example of a stray reference; the deed was a mortgage whose principal property was a south Warwickshire manor (among whose deeds it survived), but the owner included a large number of other properties he owned; when he went bankrupt in 1800, the properties were dispersed.

Detailed descriptions of houses are very rare in deeds, unless property was being partitioned when the parts of the house would be specified carefully. Usually, the only information is that the property included (say) a house and a barn, stable and bakehouse. The deed is normally more useful in identifying the size or location of the croft the house stands on and giving information about the farm land (if any). The latter will indicate the economic status of the house, at least at the date of the deed; changes in the size of freeholdings are common, often as part of the wider process of 'engrossment', the creation of large farms at the expense of smaller ones.

Ownership

The ownership of a house is not always obvious from deeds, because many relate to mortgages, marriage or family settlements or 'assignments in trust'; to sort these complications out, the section in the deed dealing with the 'uses' may need to be scrutinised. Even with the most complex transactions, the recitals of previous transfers and the 'uses' will normally identify who is the real owner. The text on the outer face of a deed (the endorsement) can be particularly useful in identifying what is going on. If it says 'Conveyance by A to B in trust for C', then you can be confident that the actual owner is C. The heading of an Abstract of Title can also be helpful when it says, for example, 'Abstract of the Title of D to a messuage at Z'. The information from deeds and abstracts and the sometimes extensive details of earlier owners and tenants will add to the sequence established from other sources. As in the example above, if the owner named in one deed is identified as someone's heir or if the wives of three men jointly selling a property were sisters, then finding the will of the father, uncle, etc. will help push the story further back.[8]

Leasehold property

For houses that were held on lease, we can make a useful distinction between those that were their owner's main property but might occasionally be leased out, and those that formed part of a large or small estate and were always leased. For the former, the freehold of the house has to be traced through its title deeds or otherwise, as discussed in the previous sections. The occasional surviving lease is useful but not crucial. Many town-dwellers owned one or two houses as an investment and to pass on to their children, even though they might live in a rented house. The tenants can be identified from rate or Land Tax assessments and from the names given in the title deeds, but it is the sequence of ownership which defines the history of the house. For example, in 1758, John Dabson, victualler, bought two houses in Dead Lane, Coventry, one occupied by William Dale, the other by William Sadler. In 1769 he left them equally to his three sons who in due course sold them off separately.[9]

For leasehold houses belonging to an estate, the changing ownership of the estate itself has little direct relevance to individual houses. Instead, the leases and estate records will be most useful in working out the house history. Typical leases of farms or houses were for set terms, especially twenty-one years (sometimes seven years). An alternative (particularly common in South-west England) was the 'three life' lease lasting for the lives of three named people, or for 99 years, if any of them should live so long.[10] For these leases the tenant always had to pay a large entry fine but then the annual 'reserved' rent was a token sum, sometimes even the same amount that had been paid as a medieval copyhold rent; leases 'in reversion' might be granted on paying a further fine, to include one or two additional lives after the death of the same number of those originally named.

Farm or cottage leases generally give little information about houses beyond there being a 'messuage' or a cottage as part of the property;[11] sometimes the entry fine for a long lease was remitted or reduced in consideration of the tenant building or rebuilding the house, whose size and character would be described. Exceptionally, leases gave much more detail, as in Seaton, Devon where they repeated the contents of an early seventeenth century survey. Thus, a lease dated 1 October 1649 described the house: *a hall and chamber over, a parlour and chamber over, a buttrie and chamber over, a dayrie or milkhouse on the south side of the buttery, a kitchen, a stable, a little low room comonly called the stall.*[12] Leases for cottages belonging to a small estate in the suburbs of Exeter give remarkably detailed information, apparently because the buildings had been destroyed during the siege of Exeter in the Civil War. For example, a lease of 1657 described one property as 'those old walls' that had been three houses and three gardens. By 1701, this had become:

> a tenement containing one ground room 22 ft long and 17 ft broad, with two chambers over, a cottage 20 ft long and 20 ft broad, and a herb garden 63 ft long and 17 ft broad, being the nearest of three dwelling houses built by William Skirrett towards the City of Exeter, part of the Manor of Bowhill.[13]

Thus, it is always worthwhile looking at any surviving leases in case they are unexpectedly informative, as well as for their evidence about the tenants.

Building Leases

Although the leases just described sometimes required tenants to undertake building work, they are very different from the building leases that were granted for the development of town streets and squares in, for example, London and Bath. These were normally for 99 years, sometimes in the form of 'head leases' of a group of building plots that would then be individually sub-let. These leases can be very informative about the building process as well as about individual houses; they frequently include plot plans and can give a timetable for construction and a detailed specification for the building; sometimes they refer to drawn-out plans or elevations, though these may not survive.

It is worth looking closely at the people who took up these leases. They were generally building craftsmen of one sort or another, rather than the ultimate occupiers of the houses. It has been noted that in Bath for example, groups of houses were leased to craftsmen with different skills, a mason, carpenter, plasterer, etc. It is clear that they were working as a co-operative, using their different skills on each house in turn.[14]

In looking for such leases, the estate records of the actual owners are an obvious source, although they may not be very informative if a system of head- and sub-leases was used. It is also worth looking for leases relating to other houses in the same street, or even in near-by streets, because their development will often follow a common pattern.[15] For London, the Middlesex Register of Deeds (Greater London RO) includes immense numbers of leases, but the lack of a street or even a parish index makes it very difficult to find those relating to a particular house (see Case Study 3).

When the lease fell in after the 99 year period, the house might be pulled down and rebuilt by the landowner, but more often another lease was simply granted for a suitable consideration. An interesting situation arose in parts of Bath (and perhaps elsewhere) in the mid-nineteenth century when some of eighteenth-century leases expired; the heirs of the original freeholder could not be discovered and the City Council assumed ownership by default. Their new leases imposed a condition that the shape of the windows had to be changed, to improve light and ventilation. As a result, the majority of Bath houses now have nineteenth rather than eighteenth century windows.

Towns where plots for new buildings were sold as freeholds rather than being leased may be more difficult to study unless groups of title deeds can be located (see previous section). However, their builders had the same problems of cash-flow that made the 99-year lease a convenient mechanism for development. The system used in Leamington Spa, Warwickshire (and presumably elsewhere) was in effect a hybrid between a sale and a lease. The freeholder granted options to the builders to purchase individual plots for a small down-payment, with interest due on the unpaid purchase money only after 12 months, by which time the house should have been built and sold. Like building leases, these option agreements can give considerable detail about the house to be built.[16]

Rentals

Not every estate has preserved long sequences of counterpart leases; indeed, formal leases may never have been drawn up for many cottages which were occupied 'at will' (in fact often for the life of the tenant). Series of rentals are an equally useful way to trace occupiers, though they do not give the detail about the property found in the leases themselves. Until the nineteenth century, it was not uncommon for rents to be unchanged for hundreds of years, with improvements in the estate income coming from increases in entry fines rather than in rents.

Fig. 5.1: A Copy of Court Roll, for Combrook, Warwickshire in 1737. The distinctive features are the name of the manor in the top left corner, the details of the court, top centre, and the information about the court record in the lower part, here the request by Ann Clark to be admitted to her third of a house and three yardlands in Combrook, following the death of her father. (SBTRO DR165/478/6)

Less obviously, rentals may also be useful for freehold property (as discussed in Chapter 4). Annual quit rents (sometimes known as chief rents or fee farm rents) were often paid by freeholdings, though by the eighteenth century, they had often either been bought out or their collection had been abandoned because it was not worth the effort. In towns, burgage rents are similar in character. Rentals giving this information should be looked at very closely, as they may be the best (or indeed the only) way to establish a sequence of owners for freeholdings.

Copyhold property

Copyhold property was held from the lord of the manor by what was essentially a medieval form of tenure, which was recorded on the manor court rolls. The medieval 'customary' villein tenure (holding according to the custom of the manor) developed into the tenure known as *copyhold*, because the tenant received a *copy* of the entry on the roll to prove his tenancy; if the manor was surveyed, he was expected to produce this copy at the special manorial court of survey. This form of tenure was gradually replaced from the sixteenth century onwards, either by leasehold (by agreement between the lord of the manor and the tenant), or by freehold by a 'deed of enfranchisement'. However, a considerable amount of property remained copyhold until the 1922 Law of Property Act enfranchised all copyholdings after 1st January 1926. Copyhold survived to a surprising extent into the eighteenth and nineteenth centuries and if any references to copyholding come to light for a particular village in this period (e.g. in the 1910 Field Books), it is quite likely that much of the property was copyhold. It is also a very encouraging discovery, much improving the chances of finding useful documentary sources. As a notable illustration, for the great manor of Taunton Deane in Somerset, almost all property in some twelve parishes around the town was held in this way and can be traced through the manorial records from 1845 back to 1550 (and sometimes earlier).[17]

Locating manorial records

One of the few genuinely straightforward steps in researching a house's history is finding the relevant manorial documents. The Manorial Register was set up in 1926, following the abolition of copyhold tenure, because of the continuing legal importance of manorial records. That importance is by now almost extinct but the register remains an invaluable resource. It will tell you both what manors are known to exist in a particular parish, and what manorial records survive for them. Information for a few counties is accessible on-line;[18] for others the register can be consulted in person or by letter or e-mail. Additional records relating to the enfranchisement of copyholdings in and after 1926 are in the PRO.[19]

The records of manor courts are usually described as 'rolls', even though from the seventeenth century onwards (and invariably by the nineteenth century), they were recorded in court books. Sometimes the steward's papers survive, comprising drafts and memoranda from which the fair copy rolls were compiled. The copyholder is usually described as a tenant, though by the eighteenth century such property rights were essentially equivalent to freehold ownership.

Copies of court roll

The equivalent of a title deed for a copyholding is the 'Copy of Court Roll' (Fig. 5.1). They are immediately recognisable from their distinctive appearance, incorporating the name of the manor in the top left corner, the date and other details of the court in the top centre, and the information from the court roll at the base. The most obvious difference from a normal title deed is that the primary record is the court roll rather than the deed. Thus, finding 'deeds' for copyhold property does not have to rely on the survival and location of the copies of court roll, but can be achieved much more straightforwardly by searching the original rolls (as in Case Study 2, a house for which no *copies* of court roll survive).

Court roll entries

Court roll entries relating to property are of two main types, outlined here.[20] The most important is the *Surrender* to a specified *use*. The copyholder surrendered the property into the lord's hands, and the new owner was then admitted, to hold it according to the custom of the manor. The crucial features on those manors where copyhold became the dominant type of land-holding lay in these customs, firstly in allowing the surrendering tenant to specify the next owner, and secondly in keeping the rent and entry payment fixed. On other manors, the rent or the fine (or both) could be increased at the lord's will, and the incoming tenant was at the lord's choice, apart from succession by children to their parent's holding; thus, the holding could be passed to whoever would pay the largest entry fine; this made copyhold almost equivalent to leasehold which generally replaced it on these manors in the sixteenth or seventeenth centuries.

By the eighteenth century, *Surrendering to uses* had become so sophisticated that the uses could include those to be specified in the future in the owner's will, or the surrender could be to a mortgagee (and would be void if the mortgage was repaid), or to the trustees of a marriage or family settlement.

The second and simpler type of court roll entry is an *Admission*. It records the death of a tenant, the succession of his widow or heir and the payment of the *heriot* (a sum due on the death of a tenant, often one year's rent). By manorial custom, a widow could generally remain in occupation of the holding unless she re-married (the widow's *freebench*); very occasionally, a widower could retain his late wife's holding in the same way.

Enfranchisement

From the seventeenth century onwards, copyhold was frequently converted to freehold by means of a *Deed of Enfranchisement*, in which the annual copyhold rent and the occasional entry fines were bought out for a lump sum In 1926, all remaining copyholds were compulsorily extinguished in this way. It is therefore not uncommon for property that was freehold in the nineteenth century formerly to have been copyhold and thus traceable through manorial records (see Case Study 2).

Locating court roll entries

Nineteenth century manor court books generally include name indexes. Thus, knowing the name of the copyholder at one date, it is easy to find his admissions and to identify those relevant to a particular property. Helpfully, the details of the preceding surrender will identify the previous tenant (and indeed often include the date of the previous copyhold grant); if this is omitted, or there is a gap in the sequence of surviving records, then entries have to be scanned to pick up the trail. The name of the person admitted is often noted in the margin of the roll.

As a striking but by no means unique example, the sequence of entries identified for a late medieval house in Knowle, Warwickshire can be cited (Case Study 2). It had a distinctive name, and a map of 1806 showed that it belonged to a wealthy local family, but one which had not left extensive estate archives; a single stray lease of 1747 was identified using the property name. After discovering that the farm had formerly been copyhold, manorial records could be used to trace the tenant families back to 1475.

Manorial records for freeholders

Even though the succession or transfer of a freeholding was not normally recorded in the manor court, the court rolls may still be useful for these properties. An inheritance payment might be due from a freeholder (a *relief* rather than the copyholder's or leaseholder's *heriot*) and this could be noted in the roll; an owner often held copyhold as well as freehold land, so its sale or his death would be recorded. He might also appear in the court rolls for any of the miscellaneous reasons that apply equally to copyholders: named in the abuttals of other property, as a manorial juror or in breach of manorial by-laws. Thus, for freeholders as well as copyholders, working through a good run of court rolls is likely to be rewarding, though it is certainly onerous.

Other Individual Documents

Fire Insurance Records

The existence of a fire-mark on a building (Fig. 5.2) can lead to valuable and unusual evidence.[21]   In the eighteenth century, many larger houses and industrial premises were insured with one of the big insurance companies. If the mark is not a replica or a 'collector's item' then, for the Sun Fire Office only, a stamped number on the mark identifies the original policy number for insuring the house. Policy records survive for this company from 1710 to 1863 in the Guildhall Library, London, so the relevant details can be obtained. In the case of the house whose fire mark is shown in Fig. 5.2, the policy number 182808 identified a policy taken out by Samuel Malkin of Coventry on 29th May 1761 for a house in his own occupation, brick and tiled, valued at not more than £100. Clearly the existing house had been built by this date and, indeed, the

Fig. 5.2: Sun Insurance Company fire insurance plaque on a house in Kenilworth, Warwickshire. The policy number on the plaque allowed the details of the policy to be identified and a date assigned to the house. (Photo: N. W. Alcock)

insurance may have been taken out when the house was finished.[22]   The Guildhall Library also has some indexes by person or place, so it may be worth searching for an entry if your house is fairly substantial, or if it carries a fire-mark from another company which lacks the policy number. Fire insurance policies themselves are also not uncommon in deed bundles.

Victuallers' Recognisances and Licenses

If you think your house used to be an inn or alehouse, then the *Victuallers' Recognisances* are a valuable source. From 1552, anyone wanting to keep an alehouse had to get a license from the Justices of the Peace and give a bond to ensure that it was kept in an orderly fashion; these are the *Recognisances* (a legal word for bond). The bonds had to be renewed annually and they survive among Quarter Sessions records, from the early eighteenth century onwards and sometimes earlier.[23]   Each individual recognisance gives the name of the licensee, the parish, the names of his sureties and (sometimes) the name of the inn. Because the bonds were taken out annually, it is easy to build up a closely dated sequence of occupier's names. Their particular value is that they pre-date the Land Tax assessments, giving information for a period often otherwise sparsely documented. However, because they do not often name the premises concerned, you will generally need to check through all the documents for the parish concerned, to discover how many inns it had and work out sequences of names for each one. By linking this information to other sources, you can relate it to the house you are studying.

A change in the law in 1828 led to the abandonment of the bond system, and from then until 1872, information on licensed premises is sparse. After the latter date, registers of licenses had to be kept and have generally survived. These registers usually identify the premises reasonably clearly.

SPECIAL TYPES OF HOUSE

The types of houses for which title deeds are not likely to be very useful include former rectories and vicarages, churches, chapels, schools, toll houses, canal buildings and railway stations. They all share one characteristic, that they once belonged to large organisations and have been sold off when surplus to requirements. After the sale, of course, title deeds can be used in the ways outlined above but, before this, research will normally need to focus on the history of the organisation itself and its records. For proposed canals, roads and railways, plans and schedules of landowners had to be deposited with Clerks of the Peace and are found among Quarter Sessions records in CROs. The PRO and the House of Lords RO also contain extensive records for canals and railways.[24]   The sale deeds for toll houses in the later nineteenth century were also regularly enrolled with Quarter Sessions. School records can be extensive (mainly in CROs) and can include details of buildings, especially if grants were requested for their erection.[25]

Parsonage houses rarely have early deeds, though occasionally deeds for land purchase may be held by diocesan offices (sometimes in ROs). However, church property including houses was described in detail in the series of Glebe Terriers, dating from the early seventeenth onwards; these are discussed in Chapter 7.   Other documentation among diocesan records may include faculty papers, visitation records and rebuilding plans (cf. Fig. 7.1).

For non-conformist chapels, licensing and registration was required at various periods, via either Quarter Sessions or the Diocese and so records indicating the existence of a chapel may survive. In 1852, these registrations were collected by the Registrar General and are now in PRO class RG31. Another important series in the PRO covers deeds for property held on trust, required to be enrolled from 1735 to 1925, which also covers some schools as well as chapels. Until 1903, these are found in class C54 and thereafter in J18.[26]

Medieval Sources

Obtaining evidence relating to individual houses from medieval documents is likely to suffer from several problems. The most obvious is that of finding documents at all. Although very many medieval documents survive, principally (for our purposes) deeds and manorial documents, they certainly do not exist for every village. Manorial records can be located in the Manorial Register (see above), but deeds need to be searched out. The best chance of finding a good collection is if the manor (rather than the parish) belonged to a major estate in the post-medieval period which may have retained early documents. If it was monastic property in the medieval period, then the PRO might hold deeds, while for a town, the borough archives are the first place to search. However, medieval deeds have become widely scattered, so the search may need to be extensive.[27]

An even more serious problem is that of relating those documents that have been found to a specific building. Success is only reasonably likely if the house has a distinctive name (perhaps an isolated farm in south-west England), or has a superior status, perhaps as the manor house. In the latter case, a question still needs to be answered: was it the original manor house, or (as is not uncommon) was a new manor house built, perhaps leaving the original one to become an ordinary farmhouse? For village houses without individual names, success in relating medieval documents to existing buildings is only likely if very extensive evidence exists, so that all the houses in the village can be identified. Research in towns is often much easier, as properties were relatively clearly described by their street and the owners of the adjoining houses. Even so, you usually need to assemble all the available information for the whole of the street before specific deeds can be correlated with house sites.

Very occasionally individual houses are immediately recognisable in the documents, as happened for a mill in Stoneleigh, Warwickshire, standing in a field that was called Robcroft on early maps. A deed dated 10th September 1490 was discovered during a systematic collection of medieval evidence for the village, which referred to the building of a water mill and miller's house in this same croft. (Fig. 5.3). This deed could therefore be related to the existing late medieval house on the site.[28]

The final problem with using medieval sources is the technical difficulty of understanding both the texts and their implications. Some collections of title deeds are well described in record office catalogues or have even been printed as texts or abstracts, but even so you probably need to compare this information with the original, in case something has been left out or mis-read. Thus, specialist skills are likely to be needed for research in the medieval period. However, by the time you have carried your research back through the eighteenth, seventeenth and sixteenth centuries, you should be well on the way to acquiring these skills.

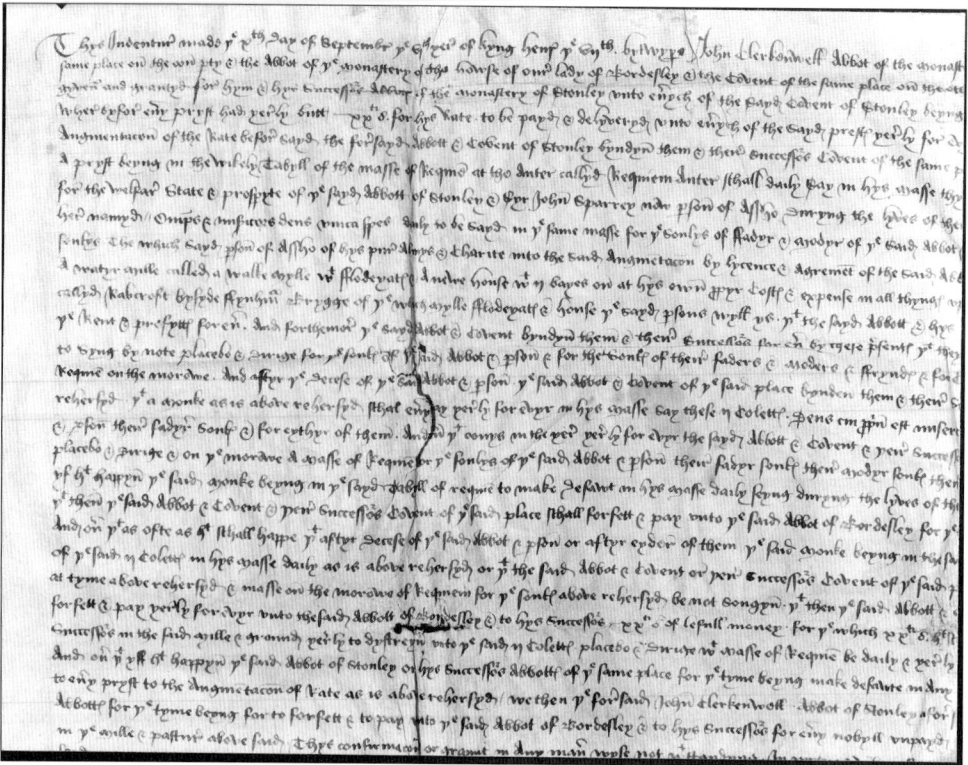

Fig. 5.3: Description of a new-built house and mill in Stoneleigh, Warwickshire,
from a deed of 1490 (SBTRO DR10/996).
Line ten gives the description of the mill and 'newe house with ij bayes'.

1   If you succeed in finding them, do make sure they are safe for the future, at the local RO.
2   See N W Alcock, *Old Title Deeds*, 2nd ed., Phillimore, 2001, p. 75.
3   For their location, see A. J. Camp, *Wills and their whereabouts*, the author, 1974.
4   Or no information at all, as registration is usually only carried out when ownership changes. Much property, mostly belonging to major landowners, still remains unregistered, because no transaction requiring it to be registered has take place.
5   This copy can be obtained by anyone, irrespective of the ownership of the property. Access information and fees are given on the Land Registry web site, *http://www.landreg.gov.uk*. If the property cannot be easily identified by a street address, you will need to send a copy of a large-scale map, so that the title number can be identified by the Registry.
6   Excluding mortgage deeds and any deeds which may have been reclaimed by the registered proprietor of the property.
7   The different legal system in Scotland from that in England, Wales and Ireland means that Scottish deeds are different in form, but the critical sections to be identified remain those relating to property description and ownership.
8   Prior to the Married Women's Property Act of 1882 (45-46 Victoria c.75), the law of *couverture* meant that on marriage, all property belonging to a woman was deemed to belong to her husband. Sometimes, to avoid this, property was left by will to trustees who held it for the use of the wife alone.
9   A small group of stray deeds running from 1627 to 1793 relate to the two properties, Birmingham Central Library, deeds within the series mss 240817 to 240861.

10   The 'lives' were those of named people living when the lease was granted. The lease was not, of course, expected to last for the full 99 years and in the eighteenth century, estate stewards reckoned that on average they would run for about 60 years.

11   The terms *messuage* and *tenement* were generally used as equivalents, sometimes together, to refer to any property; *overland tenement* referred to land leased or sold that did not include a house.

12   Somerset RO DD/WO, Boxes 29-31.

13   Cornwall RO, CF2521 (1658 assignment reciting the original 1657 lease); CF2572 (1701).

14   W Ison, *The Georgian Buildings of Bath* Kingsmead, 1980 p. 148. I am not aware of any surviving documents describing how their work was organised and paid for; such evidence would be most interesting to illustrate the building process in action.

15   Camden Local Studies and Archive Centre holds a series of deeds for the development of Red Lion Square in the 1690s by the entrepreneur Nicholas Barbon (ref JM10/3A). For another example, see Sylvia Collier with Sarah Pearson, *Whitehaven 1660-1800*, HMSO, 1991.

16   N W Alcock, 'The Building of Clarendon Crescent: 1830-1840', *Warwickshire History*, 10(6) (Winter 1998/9), 213.

17   See Derek Shorrocks, *Your Somerset House: A Guide to Tracing the History of Your House in the Somerset Record Office*, 1998.

18   Via the National Register of Archives web site (*www.nra.gov.uk*). Currently, Hampshire, Norfolk, Yorkshire and Wales are covered; other counties are being added, but progress is regrettably slow.

19   Establishing compensation for the value of the copyhold was under the charge of the Ministry of Agriculture. The PRO classes MAF9 and MAF20 contain records for many manors including deeds, court rolls and evidence of ownership of manorial rights.

20   For more detail see, for example, N W Alcock, *Old Title Deeds*, 2nd edition, Phillimore, 2001, p.94f.

21   For a local study, see H Halls, 'Fire marks and plates in Huntingdonshire' *Records of Huntingdonshire* 1(6) (1971) 89-95

22   Deeds in private hands show that he acquired the house in 1758, and a 1796 mortgage by his son (another Samuel) included a 'new erected messuage built by Samuel Malkin, deceased'.

23   See J Gibson and J Hunter, *Victuallers' licenses, records for family and local historians*, Federation of Family History Societies, 1997

24   See N Barratt, *Tracing the History of your House*, PRO, 2001, p. 158.

25   The building plans are held in CROs, while the original applications are in the PRO, class ED103 (141 vols; index in ED103/141). A small number of plans that were not transferred to CROs are in ED228.

26   They have a special index. See R W Ambler, 'Enrolled trust deeds – a source for the history of nineteenth-century nonconformity', *Archives*, 20 (1993), p. 177.

27   N W Alcock, *Old Title Deeds*, 2nd edition, Phillimore, 2001, p. 31f gives further suggestions on locating deeds both medieval and post-medieval.

28   See N W Alcock, *People at Home*, Phillimore, 1993, p. 26.

Much Parkestreete ward.

Name	Hearths	Exempt notes
~~ : ~~ Esq	11	
John Hood	1	
Thomas Webb	3	
John Yorke	2	
Henry Musson		6 pull downe 13 refused ~~ for all
John Joynes	3	
Fran: Garvis		2 prisoner in his howse
Edward Grovenor	6	
John Basnott	5	
Thomas Jesson	11	
Luke Whitley	2	
Sarah Thompson		1 dort
Thomas Smyth	0	3 no dept:
Joseph Haseldon		2 Em:
George Eylor		2 } dort:
Isaack Losson		2
George Babb	7	
Wm Ashmore		1 dort
Wm Blackwell	6	3 3 taken downe
And a pub: Oven	1	
Susan Sawloofer		1 dort
Isaack Prior	2	
Nathan: Allsop	6	
Elinor Little		1 dort
John Little	1	
Joan Higham		1 Emp:
Rich Gregory	1	
And a forge	1	

Fig. 6.1: Section of a Hearth Tax list for Much Park Street Ward, Coventry in 1666, with the numbers of hearths paying the tax in the left-hand column, the exempt hearths on the right. It shows how the rich and poor were intermingled along the street. (PRO E179/209, f. 8)

6. Living in the House

Once the names of the owners and occupiers of the house have been established, they can be studied in depth, and this chapter examines the sources available to round out the picture, to understand their social context and reveal their lifestyle. Many of the types of document described have already been mentioned in the preceding chapters but here their social evidence is primarily considered. Sometimes specific evidence for the house you are researching is sparse or even non-existent. In that case, to understand something of the life that was led within its walls, you will need to look at information relating to the same sort of house, such as probate inventories with similar rooms listed to those you suspect your house to have included, or newspaper advertisements for houses in the same area. These and other sources that help build up a general picture of lifestyles are considered in the next chapter.

Social context

A key question for any house is its place within the local community. In a village, was it a farmhouse, a craftsman's house or a labourer's cottage? If a farm, then how much land did it have *and* how does this compare with other farms in the parish? Of course, you also need to consider how the answers to these questions have changed with time. The economic framework of towns is different, but the questions are similar. Was the house built for (or occupied by) professionals, master craftsmen, tradesmen, or the poor? Did it have a dual role as a shop or workshop as well as a house? How does it compare to houses in the same street or in the same area of the town?

The answers to most of these questions will come from the sources discussed in the previous chapters, but from different aspects of their evidence to that used for identifying owners and constructing the sequence of occupiers. Status or profession is usually included in deeds or leases, but may need to be supplemented from other sources. Tithe maps and Land Tax assessments show individual properties in their community framework (subject to the caveats about the loose relationship between assessments and actual value mentioned in Chapter 4). Hearth Tax lists (Fig. 6.1) are particularly useful They give simple information about the economic standing of individual houses, but also give an overview of the parish or town as a whole, revealing the balance between large and small houses and between the prosperous payers of the tax and their poorer exempt neighbours. In Case Study 2 (p. 74), the four-hearth assessment is among the largest in the parish, suggesting a rather higher status for the house than its size might indicate.

Building evidence

The Hearth Tax

As well as indicating the standing of a house in relation to its neighbours, the number of hearths in a house is also directly informative about its development and functioning as a building. It can also be compared to the existing structure. A house in Lapworth, Warwickshire with what was obviously an original pair of back-to-back fireplaces (and with a third hearth upstairs) paid the 1674 Hearth Tax for just one hearth. This reinforced a conclusion based on structural comparisons that it had been rebuilt after this date.

Building plans

From the mid-nineteenth century onwards, plans for buildings in many towns had to be approved by a committee of the local council and these have survived in large numbers in some ROs (Fig. 6.2). Birmingham City Archives, for example, has some 250,000 plans dating from 1859 onwards. Rural house-plans tend to survive (if at all) only from much later. Although in these plans you may find evidence for alterations to an earlier house, they are particularly useful for proposed new houses – though one must remember that the

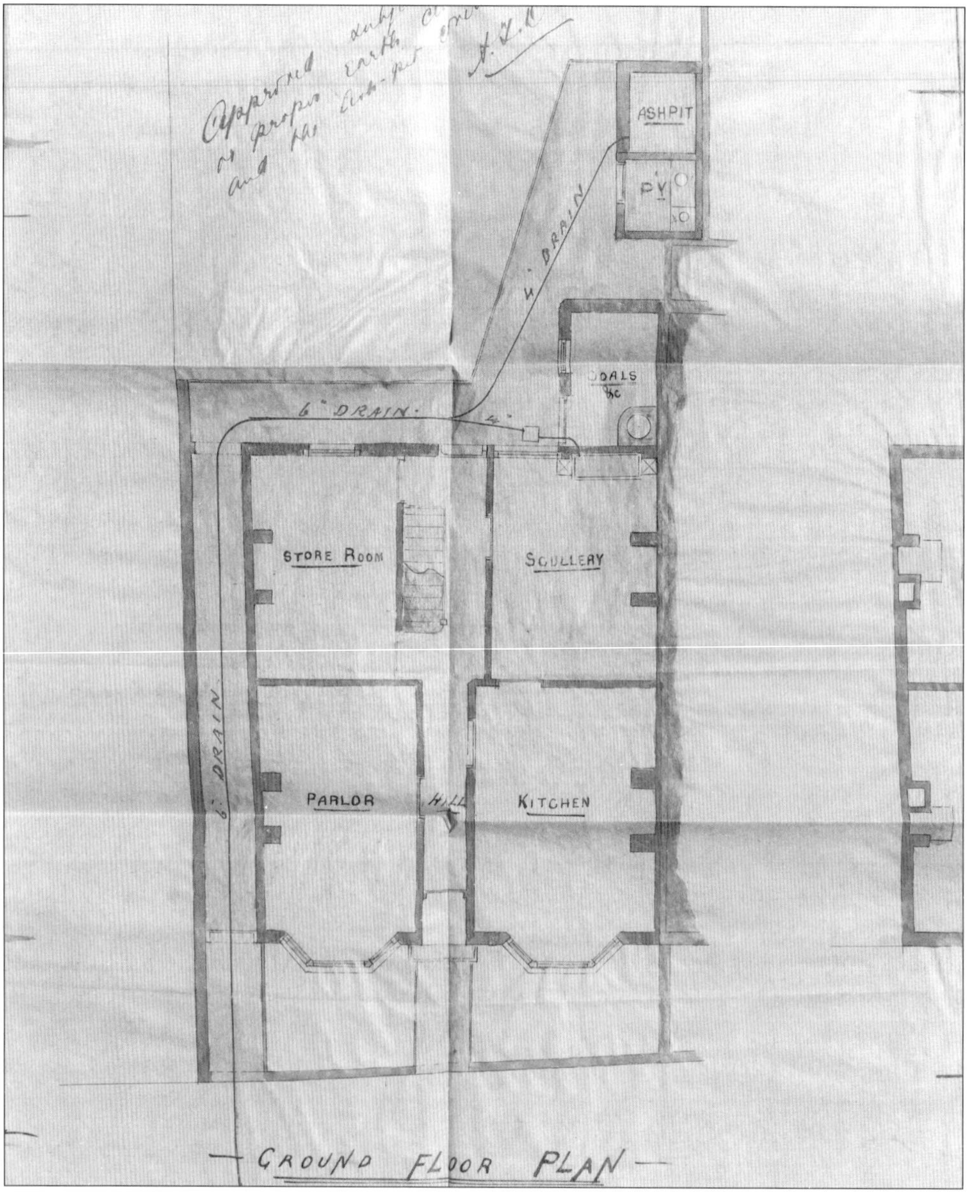

Fig. 6.2: A building plan submitted for bye-law approval in Stratford-upon-Avon in 1883
(SBTRO BRR 49/1/82)

project may not always have been carried out. Obviously, they give good evidence for the building date and the plan or the corresponding register will name both the 'architect' (sometimes merely the builder or his draftsman) and the owner. Usually, though not always, they identify the rooms in the house but, especially if this information is missing, it is worth looking at some other plans for nearby houses of the same date. These will show how typical your plan was and help identify the rooms.

Land Agent's records

If you are fortunate enough to be working in a county for which an extensive series of Land Agent's records survive (Chapter 7), you may get valuable information if they include your house. For south Warwickshire, the Margetts notebooks are indexed by parish, with the reference including the name of the tenants and/or owner. Thus, once the name of a tenant is known, it is easy to discover useful entries. The entries may be simply the valuation of crops for a Michaelmas change of tenant, but they often include valuations of tenant's fixtures which incidentally provide a list of the rooms (Fig. 6.3).

Other lists of rooms

In favourable cases, probate inventories (discussed below) list house contents room by room. If you are not fortunate enough to find one directly related to your house, those for other houses in or near the parish can identify the local room names used and perhaps indicate typical layouts. Sale catalogues and newspaper advertisements (if either exist) also generally include the names of rooms. The Field Books from the 1909-10 Valuation give a summary of the rooms in the house and the farm buildings, and in many cases include layout diagrams of the farm (Fig. 6.4). All these sources will add to the evidence for both the physical development of the house through the centuries and for the changing descriptions given to its rooms.

For church property, not only rectories and vicarages but also farms belonging to the church, glebe terriers provide either lists of rooms or summaries of the size of the house in bays. They are discussed fully in Chapter 7.

Families

The same sources that identify occupiers' names often give more information, such as craft or social status. For tenants, the three-life leases used on some estates (p. 30) are useful, identifying several family members or relatives, while surveys of estates often include the ages of the 'lives' and sometimes other telling comments. Thus, for a farm valued at £47 19s in Nettlecombe, Somerset in 1619, the comment was added 'The old stickes is of opinion that it is worth but £45 10s'.[1] Caution is needed because the actual occupier may be sub-letting the house from the tenant named in the estate records; it is important if possible to get confirmation from different sources, for example, Land Tax or Hearth Tax returns.

In general, information on occupiers will come from standard sources for family history (see Further Reading), especially parish registers, census returns, wills and memorial inscriptions.[2] For the nineteenth century, census returns identify family members, but also include the domestic and farm servants, sometimes in surprising ways. Thus, Thomas Wathes, a farmer and milkman in Edgbaston, Birmingham, was listed as employing eight men and boys for his 65 acre farm, an unexpectedly large number. The census gives the family and two living-in servants, one for the household and one a farm

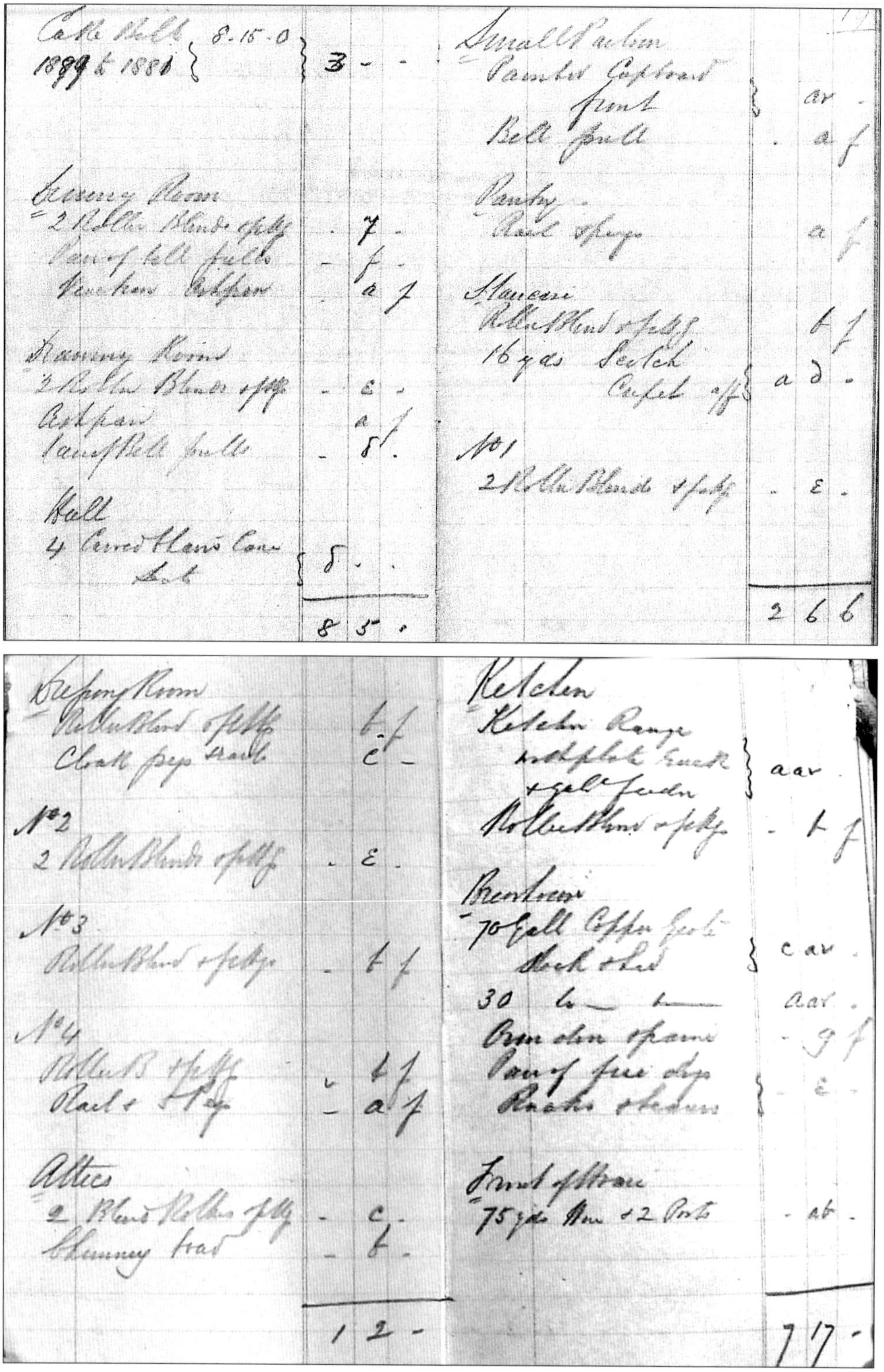

Castle Hill 8-15-0
1889 to 1881 3 - -

Dressing Room
2 Roller Blinds & fittings
Pair of bell pulls
Kitchen Ashpan

Drawing Room
2 Roller Blinds & fittings
Ashpan

Hall
4 Carved Chairs Cane Seat

8 5 -

Small Parlour
Painted Cupboard front
Bell pull

Pantry

Staircase
Roller Blind & fittings
16 yds Scotch Carpet

No 1
2 Roller Blinds & fittings

2 6 6

Dressing Room
Roller Blind & fittings

No 2
2 Roller Blinds & fittings

No 3
Roller Blind & fittings

No 4

Attics
2 Blind Rollers & fittings
Chimney bar

1 2 -

Kitchen
Kitchen Range

Roller Blind & fittings

Front of House
75 yds

7 17 -

Fig 6.3: Pages from a land agent's notebook, valuing tenant's fixtures in a house in Priors Marston, Warwickshire in 1881. The valuations are given in a simple code (a = 1, etc.). This is the second of two pages, starting with the dressing room for bedroom No. 1 (WCRO CR2433/31/232, p. 20) labourer. It also lists four young men, all born in Ireland, who were sleeping in the barn. Although described as farm labourers, they may well also have worked on the milk round.

Parish registers, wills and tombstones establish the family relationships of the owners and tenants, and it is notable how often apparently unconnected tenants are in fact linked. At the Edgbaston farm just mentioned, the early nineteenth century tenants were successively John Pritchatt (1816-1837) and his son Joseph Lilley Pritchatt (1837-1863). As we might expect, John's wife was Sarah Lilley. Her father, William Lilley, and his father John before him were the tenants of the same farm from 1789 to 1815. Often, no doubt, the son-in-law would take over the running of the farm as the father became elderly and would either succeed to the tenancy or be the obvious person for the estate to pick as a new tenant.

On occasion, in pursuing a family history, suspected links can be elusive. Documents such as family or marriage settlements can sometimes come to light in the context of property history that would have been very difficult to locate starting from the family. A good illustration is given by Case Study 2, where court roll entries established the relationship between successive copyhold farm tenants.

Lifestyles

The plan and layout of a house gives clues about the original use of its rooms, from the locations of doors, fireplaces and other fittings, and the quality of the decoration. Comparison with other houses in the region can help identify typical plans for the relevant period,[3] but it is less easy to discover more about how the house was lived in. Successive census listings will show how many people used the house. They may highlight the decreasing importance of living-in farm or domestic servants, and sometimes show that houses with elderly owners or tenants were surprisingly empty.

Probate and other Inventories

For detailed evidence on life in your house between the sixteenth and the eighteenth centuries, probate inventories are by far the best source (Fig. 6.5). A probate inventory is a list of goods with their values taken as part of the administration of a deceased person's estate, and good examples can go into very great detail. Having an inventory associated with a specific house gives extra insights both into the house and the inventory, as illustrated in Case Study 5. Unfortunately, making this association is only possible for a minority of houses. Finding an inventory for a specific house depends on establishing the sequence of occupiers, and then having the good fortune that some of them died while in occupation. Sometimes it seems that this never happened, perhaps because the house was let on a series of short tenancies. Often what is lacking, though, is the evidence to link the inventories to specific houses. The next chapter discusses how inventories can still be used as general evidence and also how and where to find them.

As an example of what can be achieved, in the Warwickshire village of Stoneleigh, some 24 houses survive from the eighteenth century or earlier, out of an total of about 45 holdings.[4] Estate records have allowed almost complete sequences of tenants to be built up for each house, covering the two centuries from about 1550 onwards. Inventories can be identified relating to sixteen of the standing houses, and also to the same number where the house has disappeared. Contrary to the normal expectation, the smaller houses survive unusually well in this village, but it is primarily these to which no inventories can be related. Thus, even with such an abundance of evidence, life in a proportion of the houses has to be described in generalisations.

Not uncommonly, a probate inventory was drawn up room by room, with the result that it can be correlated with the house being researched. A probate inventory that gives

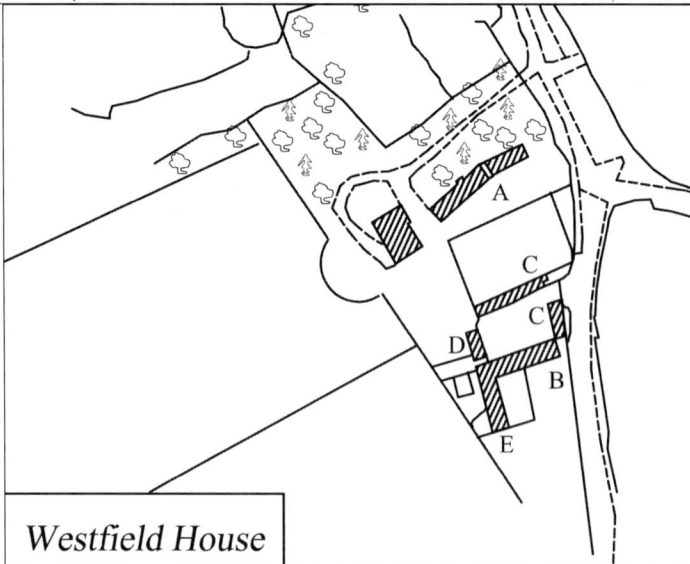

Fig. 6.4: 1910 'Domesday' Field Book for hereditament 30 in Prior's Marston, Warwickshire, showing two of the four pages relating to the property; the farm layout has been re-traced for clarity. For the corresponding map, see Fig. 3.2. (PRO IR58/89460).

serve form 7   Reference No. 30...........

Particulars, description, and notes made on inspection 29/4/13.

A useful pasture farm in Priors Marston Village, with a large, plain but substantially built house, and adequate outbuildings. The house (approached by a small drive) is stone slated, old, & contains:- on 2nd floor 5 Bedrooms on 1st floor 4 Bedrooms, boxroom & bathroom, on ground floor Drawing room, dining room, breakfast room, outer & inner hall, lavatory, kitchen pantry cellars & w.c. Fences & Water good

Charges, Easements, and Restrictions affecting market value of Fee Simple

Valuation.— Market Value of Fee Simple in possession of whole property.

in its present condition	37..0	*Annual rental*	~~235~~ 250	
Repairs etc 15%	35 X 0	*outgoings say*	~~41~~ 44	
Land tax	5 14 4		~~194~~ 206	
Tithe	0 14 0		41 ~~35~~ 28 2	
	41 13 4	*Timber*	4850 5871	
	41		220 250	
			£ ~~5070~~ 6100 *say*	

Deduct Market Value of Site under similar circumstances, but if divested of structures, timber, fruit trees, and other things growing on the land

       @ £23 per acre   say. £ ~~2950~~ 3860

Difference Balance, being portion of market value attributable to structures, timber, &c. .... £ ~~2120~~ 2240

Divided as follows:—

Buildings and Structures..................... £ 1760.
Machinery .... £
Timber.. £ 220.
Fruit Trees .... £ 5
Other things growing on land .... £ ~~135~~ 255

Market Value of Fee Simple of Whole in its present condition (as before) .... £ ~~5070~~ 6100

Add for Additional Value represented by any of the following for which any deduction may have been made when arriving at Market Value:—

Charges (excluding Land Tax).......... say. £ 20
Restrictions... *footpath, bridle, road* ..... £ 40   £ 60

GROSS VALUE... £ ~~5130~~ 6160

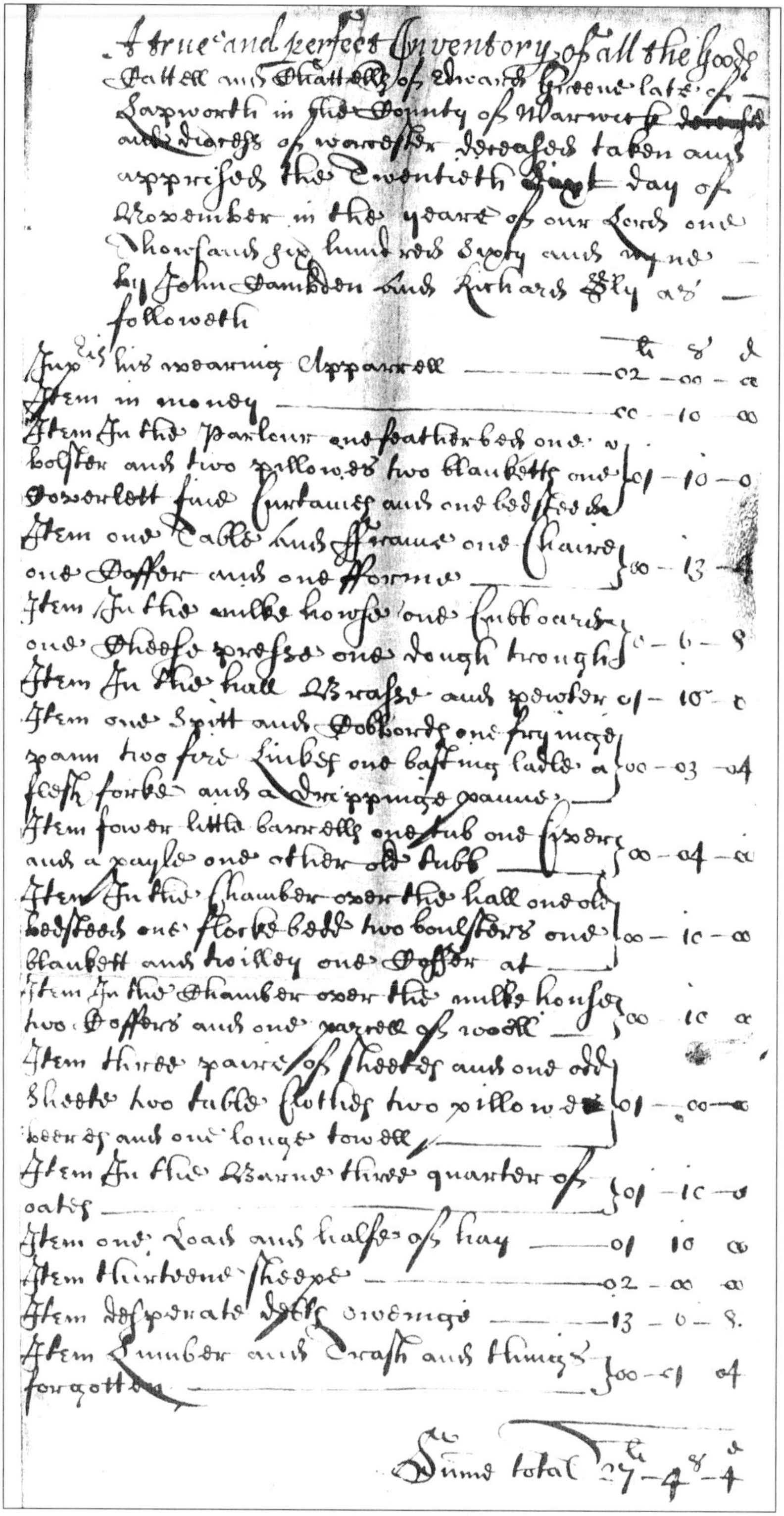

A true and perfect Inventory of all the goods Cattell and Chattells of Edward Greene late of Lapworth in the County of Warwick and diocess of worcester deceased taken and apprised the Twentieth first day of Novembr in the yeare of our Lord one Thousand six hundred sixty and nyne by John Dambden and Richard Sly as followeth

	li	s	d
Impris his wearing Apparrell	02	00	00
Item in money	00	10	00
Item In the parlour one feather bed one bolster and two pillowes two blanketts one Coverlett five Curtaines and one bedstead	01	10	0
Item one Table and frame one Chaire one Coffer and one fforme	00	13	4
Item In the milke house one Cubboarde one Cheese presse one dough trough	0	6	8
Item In the hall Brasse and pewter	01	10	0
Item one Spitt and Cobbords one fryinge pann two fire Irons one basting ladle a flesh forke and a drippinge panne	00	03	04
Item fower little barrells one tub one sieve and a payle one other old tubb	00	04	00
Item In the Chamber over the hall one old bedsteed one flocke bedd two boulsters one blankett and coverlet one Coffer at	00	10	00
Item In the Chamber over the milke house two Coffers and one parcell of woolle	00	10	0
Item three paire of sheetes and one odd sheete two table clothes two pillowe beeres and one longe towell	01	00	00
Item In the Barne three quarter of oates	01	10	0
Item one Load and halfe of hay	01	10	00
Item thirteene sheepe	02	00	00
Item desperate debts owenge	13	0	8
Item Lumber and trash and things forgotten	00	01	04

Summe total 27li - 4s - 4d

Fig. 6.5: Probate inventory for Edward Green of Lapworth, Warwickshire in 1669 (Worcestershire RO 1669/70, no. 26).

such a room-by-room listing of the contents will show how many rooms were in the house and what was their principal use. As in the example in Case Study 5, the first step in interpretation is to compare the structure of the house, the positions of fireplaces and other features with the rooms in the inventory. Then it is useful to consider whether the sequence of rooms in the inventory represents a sensible progression through the house. If a serious mis-match emerges, the identification may need to be reconsidered, or the possibility examined that the house was rebuilt later than the date of the inventory. Next comes a consideration of what the contents of each room show about life in the house – though imagination may be needed to work back from the listing of tables and beds, or where the junk was kept, to the domestic and the farming economy. Such interpretation is always easier within the framework of other inventories from the region or the community, which will indicate what is normal and what exceptional (see Chapter 7 and Further Reading).

Inventories are fascinating documents and give the best opportunity to discover how our forbears lived, but it is important to warn those less experienced that they may be difficult both to read and to interpret. They are notorious for the unusual terms they use, and every printed collection of inventories has its own glossary. Particularly deceptive are terms that have changed their sense. Thus, neither 'bed' nor 'loom' may have their expected meanings ('bed' = mattress and 'loom' = vat).

Wills can sometimes take the place of missing inventories, as well of course as being vital for establishing family relationships. Widows, in particular, tended to distribute their possessions with great precision to numbers of relatives, identifying household goods and clothes by their location and character, 'the second best brass pot in the kitchen', for example. The combination of all the individual bequests can give a good view of the household and its lifestyle.

The Household in the Twentieth Century

Evidence about the life of the household in the twentieth century, after the 1901 census and the 1910 Valuation records, is generally much sparser than earlier. The sequence of owners and occupiers can usually be established from title deeds, directories and electoral registers. To fill in the picture, the best source is probably oral recollection, though this should be checked from other sources. The owner of one Warwickshire house for a long period in the 1930-40s was by report a champion tennis player. The existence of a run of Annual Handbooks of the Warwickshire Lawn Tennis Association suggested that the stories had been embroidered. They listed the competitors in the county championships and the past holders of their trophies, and his name was conspicuously absent.

---

1   Somerset RO DD/WO Box 43, Survey of Nettlecombe, p. 89.
2   In an increasing number of counties, tombstone inscriptions have been systematically recorded and
     lists deposited in the CRO. Once the relevant names are known, checking these lists can be
     rewarding. See Case Study 4.
3   See Chapter 2, p. 4
4   N W Alcock, *People at Home*, Phillimore, 1993.

7. The History of Housing

The preceding sections have explored documentary sources for the history of individual houses. Many of these are also informative about the changing character of housing, and give evidence about developments in building practices, building costs, house plans and lifestyles. However, if these more general topics are the objectives of your research, other sources become important. These contain evidence which might in principle be valuable for individual houses, but where correlation with a particular standing structure is almost impossible, or where the information for any one building is insignificant out of context. Beyond the scope of this book but obviously not to be neglected is the evidence of standing buildings themselves for building history.[1]

Aspects of these topics can also clearly be of interest to those more concerned with individual houses giving, for example, insights into life in medieval houses which you are unlikely to be able discover for any one house in particular. However, both locating relevant original sources and using them many be difficult without considerable experience. Thus, whenever possible, references to published studies are included below, which can be used for background information. Many papers examining such sources have appeared over the last 30 years, especially in the journal *Vernacular Architecture*; those published (up to 1994 at present) are listed in the *Bibliography of Vernacular Architecture* (see Further Reading).

Documentary sources for the history of housing in the post-medieval period fall into the three broad categories considered below: those covering groups of houses, such as surveys; those relating to individual houses but including numbers of examples, such as groups of probate inventories; those relating to specific buildings, such as contracts or building accounts. The sparse documentary sources for medieval houses are considered in the final section.

Sources for groups of houses

Maps

Early maps often include thumbnail sketches of houses but these are generally conventional images rather than pictures of specific houses. One exception has been identified, those of the Walker family of surveyors from Hanningfield, Essex. Their 34 surviving maps dating from 1584 to 1622 cover mainly estates in Essex but range as far afield as Hampshire.[2] The maps distinguish plan form (single range, hall with crosswing, etc.), construction (brick or timber framed) and roofing material (thatch or tile). Thus they give visual impressions of complete villages and, on one map, of a Tudor town (Chelmsford). Other estate maps, tithe maps and OS maps have little information about types of houses, but they do illustrate the layouts of farmsteads. From these plans, developments in regional farming can be followed, such as the adoption of covered yards or of the distinctive polygonal horse-engine houses which were constructed from the late eighteenth to the mid-nineteenth century.[3] The farm layouts on OS maps can be supplemented from the 1910 'Domesday' Field Books

(PRO IR58; Fig. 6.4), which in some regions include block plans of farmsteads, identifying the function of each building.

House-and-estate surveys

Estate surveys generally identify the presence of a house on a tenant holding in such terms as, 'one messuage, one garden, ...' and sometimes itemise the farm buildings, 'one barn, one stable ...', but they rarely give more information. A very few surveys (identified as *house-and-estate surveys*)[4] include descriptions of houses as well as more standard material. At their simplest, these list the numbers of bays,

> Hugh Crosse, age 80, holdith by copie granted by William Clifton, esquire, datid the 30th day of May in the first yeere of Elizabeth [1559], one tenement with a hall with other roomes of 4 couples [*bays*], a barne and a stable of 5 couples, and one farthinge of land (Kenton, Devon, 1597).[5]

More sophisticated examples may describe construction, dimensions or the numbers and names of rooms,

> John Floode senior, John Floode junior and Nicholas Floode hold: Inprimis 1 dwelling howse, 1 hall, 1 parlour, 1 mylkehowse, 1 buttery with 1 under chamber and [?5] roomes over the same, 4 cowple in length, 1 bakehouse or maulthowse 2 poole, 1 barne and 1 shyppen and 1 lynnage 4 cowple (Farway, Devon, 1609).[6]

Examples from the north of England tend to give very simple descriptions, but they are still of significance as evidence for the construction and size of houses. In Skelsmergh, Westmorland in c.1602, one Robert Harrison held:

> an awncient tenement, a fier howse, stone thakt of 3 paire of trees [*crucks*], a barne of 4 paire of trees, a cowhouse and stable...[7]

These surveys provide exceptional evidence for houses, particularly because they cover all the buildings in a particular village but they are very rare and locating them is not easy. The published lists are known to be incomplete and the only effective way to identify examples for a particular region is to examine every survey that can be found in local or national estate collections, dating between about 1550 and 1750, broadly the date range for these surveys. The largest groups which regularly contain house-and-estate surveys are the series made of the Crown Estates from about 1607 onwards (PRO, mainly in LR2), and the 1649 Parliamentary Surveys of Crown, Dean and Chapter and Bishopric estates (PRO and diocesan archives).

Despite the remarkable information given by these surveys, they have been surprisingly little exploited. A notable exception is the correlation of a 1556 survey of Ingatestone, Essex, which includes the dimensions of the housing units with the 1602 Walker map of the same estate.[8] A study of Thurleigh, Bedfordshire compared the houses described in a 1604 survey with the standing buildings.[9] An extensive study of all the known house-and-estate surveys for south-west England, including text abstracts as well as analysis, is in preparation.[10]

The Hearth Tax

Although the information in Hearth Tax assessments is limited, they do cover all the houses within each parish, hundred and county. The analysis of this evidence in relation to house types and housing standards is one of the principal objectives of a project now being undertaken by the British Record Society, to put in print the assessment for at least one year for every English county.[11] The exemplary introduction by Sarah Pearson to the first volume in the series, that on Kent,[12] shows how the numbers of hearths can be related to the character of the housing stock and to relative prosperity in the different regions of the county. Technical questions about the inclusion of those exempted from the tax need to be considered before one can be confident of the completeness of the assessments.[13] With these resolved, the assessments can be mapped to identify the variations in housing standards across a county and from county to county, revealing hitherto unsuspected variations.[14] The range of hearths in particular settlements is also significant in giving context to specific houses (Chapter 6).

Sources for numbers of houses
Glebe terriers
These summaries of church property within a parish were compiled between about 1600 and 1850, usually in relation to episcopal visitations. They are found among diocesan archives, sometimes with copies also in parish records. A number of series are in print, though none cover the full date range of surviving terriers.[15] As parsonage houses are relatively easy to locate, the terriers are invaluable for the history of these individual houses (Chapter 5); however, the house described in an early terrier will very often have been rebuilt, sometimes even on a different site. If the glebe included tenanted farms, their houses were also described, so their evidence is relevant to any house belonging to the church.

Glebe terriers generally include a description of the parsonage house as well as its land, the amount of detail depending on local practice. Thus, in timber-framing regions of the Midlands and Eastern England, only the materials and number of bays in the building may be given, though a number of eighteenth century Northamptonshire and Buckinghamshire terriers include sketch plans.[16] In the South-West, the names of the individual rooms were usually included, sometimes even with sketch plans to show their layout.[17] Thus, for example, the 1727 terrier for Clyst St Mary, Devon reads (in part)

> The parsonage house very ancient, walls made of cob or earth, roof covered with reed or thatch. It consists of four rooms below stairs and five above, all well ceiled, viz. A kitchen paved with stone, a Hall with a cob flower [*earth floor*], A Parlour plancht and wainscotted, and a cellar pavd. The five chambers are well planchd, ceiled and plastered. To the south side of the house is annext a narrow range containing a Brewhouse, a Steenhouse [*meaning uncertain*], a pantry and a cellar with three chambers over … [18]

The terriers give excellent overviews of housing standards within a region. Typically, the vicar or rector in the sixteenth and seventeenth centuries was not very well-off, and his house would be of equivalent quality to the other village houses,[19] By the eighteenth century, the vicar's income had often been supplemented by additional endowments (especially from Queen Anne's Bounty) and his house would often be rebuilt or improved; the process will be clear from the changing descriptions in the terriers.[20]

Other documentation among diocesan records may include faculty papers, visitation records and rebuilding plans. Applications for support from Queen Anne's Bounty may be accompanied by evidence about the existing house. A remarkable example of this is shown in Fig. 7.1.

Fig. 7.1: Elevation of the vicarage of Broadhempston, Devon in 1777 (accompanied by a plan),
part of a petition for its rebuilding with support from Queen Anne's Bounty. (Devon RO,
Diocesan Parsonage Houses, Devon, 27, reproduced with the permission of the
Exeter Diocesan Registrar)

Inventories

Inventories, especially those taken for probate (for the administration of a deceased person's estate), are perhaps the most significant single source for the development of housing, of lifestyles and of living standards. For individual buildings, they are of great interest but the discovery of relevant inventories can be difficult and frustrating (Chapter 6). This chapter discusses their wider application, in regional or local studies not tied to specific houses.

The great majority of inventories survive from probate administration. As this was controlled by the church, most are found among diocesan archives in local record offices associated with wills. People with property in more than one diocese had to have their wills proved in the Prerogative Courts, either of Canterbury (records in the PRO) or York (in the Borthwick Institute, York).[21]

The making of probate inventories was required from the medieval period but they only survive in significant numbers following the enactment of a statute in 1539.[22] Indeed, in many dioceses, the inventory series only start in the 1660s, after the reinstatement of the church courts that had been abolished during the Commonwealth. Inventories have continued to be made as an adjunct to probate up to the present day, but diocesan series usually fade out in the early or mid-eighteenth century. Some later examples can be found in private archive collections, and in Consistory Court records in relation to disputed probate cases.[23] Even for a general study, it is rarely worth searching out probate inventories in these other sources unless the principal series are inadequate (as for Devon, following the destruction of its probate records in 1942). Medieval inventories are rare, though the PRO holds a few hundred (in PROB2); others have to be located in private collections.

Other sources for inventories from the later nineteenth and twentieth centuries are land-agents' records (below) and catalogues for the sales of house contents. Inventories of this period are relatively rare, but it is usually easy to identify the house to which they relate, because they usually include modern house names or numbers, or the names of known occupiers.

The information provided by probate inventories varies greatly by region and sometimes even by parish. Room-by-room listing of household goods is occasionally found in the sixteenth century onwards, but more often rooms were only named in the later seventeenth century (and sometimes not even then).[24] In these circumstances, changes in wealth and lifestyle can be studied but for housing details, a large block of inventories may need to be scanned. One then needs to consider whether the few with extra details are typical of the majority. This is one aspect of a larger question: To what extent do probate inventories give an unbiased picture of their community? Comparison of the inventories with full lists of households (most obviously Hearth Tax assessments) allows the proportion of inventoried households to be determined. Bias in the sample towards more prosperous households can then be corrected.[25]

A study using probate inventories at a regional or local level might initially survey the numbers and types of rooms in houses and how this changes with date. Following that, the contents of each type of room will indicate what were the household activities and where they were located. Many series of probate inventories are in print for individual places and regions, while a number of published studies have used inventories to study buildings and lifestyles. M. W. Barley, *The English Farmhouse and Cottage* (1961) examines types of houses and their regional development, in part in the light of inventory evidence; L. Wetherill, *Consumer behaviour and material culture in Britain 1660-1760* (1988) discusses changes in lifestyle and the development of consumerism in the eighteenth century. However, the latter's restriction to post-1660 inventory series makes what I believe was a long drawn-out process of social improvement appear as a sudden innovation.

For periods before the start of probate inventory series, it is also worth looking systematically at wills. Although they only occasionally include evidence about houses, individual examples can be very informative. For example, Bennet Shuckborough of Cubbington, Warwickshire in his 1617 will instructed his grandson to leave as 'standards' (i.e. as permanent heirlooms):

> all the joyned bedsteeds in the grange house [*his house*] together wythall the glasse in the wyndowes and all the wyndowe lidds and shuttings and all the doores and lockes with keyes … and all the furniture in the haule, as tables, frames, formes, stooles … together wyth lyke furniture in the old ketchen … alwayes remayninge as standers … for the heires of the sayd Edward.[26]

Builders' records
A considerable number of RO deposits relate to builders, the majority for the later nineteenth and twentieth centuries.[27] These can cover a wide range of material, most often financial, but also including plans and other architectural material.

Local Authority building plans
As well as their use for specific buildings (Chapter 6), these plan series provide a detailed overview of the changing character of urban building from the mid-nineteenth century onwards. The principal problem in using them is probably the immense amount of material, making the identification of typical examples difficult. They are less useful for rural buildings because of the relatively late date from which they normally survive.

However, later changes may be well illustrated from this source. One of the distinctive early twentieth century 'Shack and Track' developments, involving simple houses on un-made-up roads, was developed between 1921 and 1932, and the plans from Rugby Rural District Council show the character of its buildings.[28]

Land Agents' records

For the nineteenth and early twentieth centuries, the lack of probate inventories can be compensated for by the records of land and estate agents. As an example, in south Warwickshire, almost 1,000 notebooks compiled by Margetts between 1851 and 1933 include hundreds of valuations of household fixtures for outgoing tenants or furnishings for probate (as well as many more land, crop and timber valuations) (Fig. 6.3). Thus, they provide a systematic record about housing and living standards for one particular group in rural society. I know of several similar series in other record offices and more presumably survive.[29] As well as their significance for individual houses, they offer an exceptional source for systematic information on houses in a period when many other sources are unavailable.

Sources for Individual houses

Building accounts

Post-medieval building accounts are not uncommon, mostly found in estate archives or those of corporate bodies such as boroughs. The level of detail they provide is very variable, though sometimes disappointing, concentrating on wages paid per day or week with less about the work being undertaken. However, good examples are highly informative. One for building a cottage at Kirkby Soken, Essex in 1743 describes it as 'set in the ground without sells [sills]', i. e. the type of structure normally only found in the medieval period by archaeology. The account gives enough detail to show that the house was about 13 by 20 ft in size, single storey with two rooms, roughly timber-framed and thatched and with a brick chimney and oven. It cost £10 14s.[30]

Building contracts

Building contracts survive in the same contexts as accounts, but are much rarer. However, they do generally give considerable detail about the building. Thus, an agreement of 1577 for a house at Holbrook near Ipswich, Suffolk not only includes such details as 'the planchet [*planking*] to be well planched with inch bord' and ' the hall chamber to have three windows', but has a plan showing that the house was to have a lobby-entry plan, with a hall at one end, central parlour and 'buttere' at the other end.[31] In a later example (1700) of a contract for carpenter's work, a substantial house in Fetcham, Surrey was to be built according to a 'draught' (which has not survived) and the contract goes through the required scantlings for all the timber, e.g. 'The girders to be of good yellow furr, 14 in broade and 9 in deep for all the floors except the ground floor, and the joysts for the said two upper floores with the brieeings to be of the same depth with the girder and 3 in thick.')[32]

In this case, the payment was not agreed in advance, but was to be by area at the rate of '£8 per square (*10ft by 10ft area*) that shall appeare to be on the airey or flatt of the said building according to the customary way of measurement'.

A contract of 1679 for a house in Warwickshire proved sufficiently detailed that the house could be reconstructed on paper, even though it did not survive (and indeed may not ever have been constructed).[33]

Plans and drawings

Plans and elevations of modest houses are also very common in estate collections, generally dating from the eighteenth century onwards, though occasionally earlier. The conventions used seem to show a development, the earliest examples being rather schematic with walls represented as lines and doors/windows often omitted; the example in Fig. 7.2 is unusual in identifying the doors and windows by numbers. Later drawings resemble modern examples much more closely (e.g. Fig. 7.3).[34] House plans

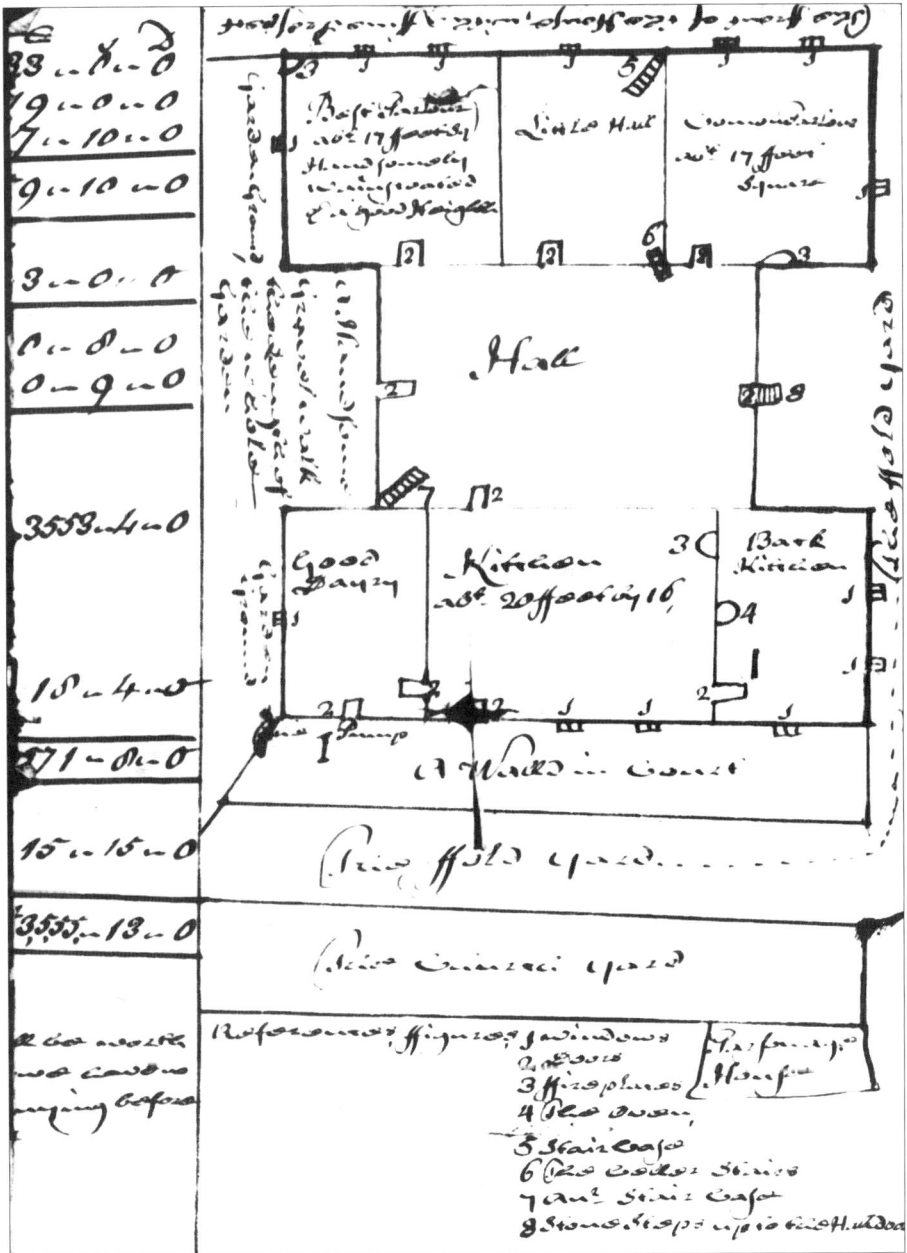

Fig. 7.2: Early seventeenth century plan of a substantial house, possibly at Colwall, Herefordshire (University of Melbourne, Bright Papers Box 72)

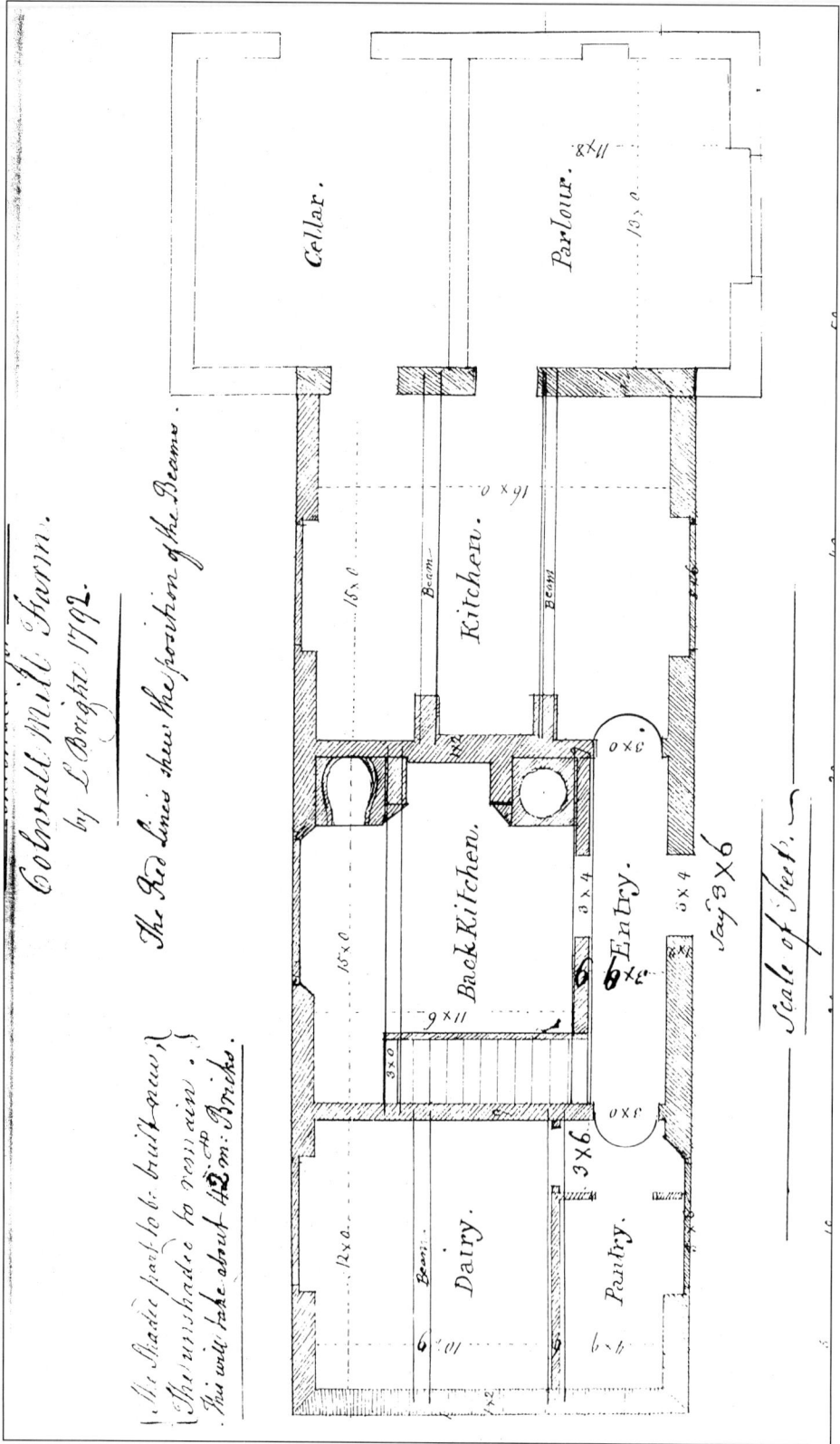

Fig. 7.3: The plan of a house in Colwall, Herefordshire, 1792 (University of Melbourne, Bright Papers Box 72)

are also occasionally found in legal papers, especially among exhibits. Thus, the PRO holds the plans and specification for a house in Crediton, Devon in 1744 (being rebuilt after the fire in the town in 1743), where the builder had died before completing the work he had contracted for. The same series also includes drawings of the vicarage of St Nicholas parish, Warwick, though it is not so obvious why they were presented to the court.[35]

Property plans in deeds and leases sometimes include internal plans of the houses, though more often they show only the plot layout. However, some series of plans do exist, of which the most notable are those drawn up by Ralph Treswell for a number of London estates in the early seventeenth century. These amazingly detailed (and advanced) drawings show both dimensions and room names in hundreds of London houses (see cover).[36]

Topographical drawings from the eighteenth century onwards are very numerous.[37] They are obviously useful in showing the development of particular houses, if relevant examples can be identified. However, for changes in housing type and standard, they are generally disappointing. The representation of buildings are not usually precise enough to identify structural types or plan forms – or the possibly significant features are plastered over. A few exceptions can be cited and local collections must include others. The drawings of the Buckler family (mainly among the manuscripts in the British Library) do include extremely detailed drawings of timber-framed houses; 1850s drawings of houses in Coventry by Nathaniel Troughton also contribute significantly to the knowledge of structures in that city.[38] The same problems also affect early photographs which, also, are normally more useful for individual buildings than for general studies.

England has not had the same tradition of interior paintings that is, for example, very marked in Flanders. Thus, early representations of interiors are almost unknown, whether in painting or manuscript.[39] Only with the development of genre painting in the nineteenth century can numbers of interiors be found, and these seem sometimes suspiciously idealised.[40] However, a few exceptions can be found, mainly in private sketchbooks, while Mary Ellen Best, a Yorkshire artist, produced interior views of her own house and of those she saw on her travels.[41]

Covenants and schedules in deeds

As well as the information on ownership and property in deeds (Chapter 5), leases in particular may include conditions about repairs or rebuilding that the tenant has to undertake.[42] Thus, a lease of 1580 for a manor house in Bedfordshire included the requirement that the tenant would within seven years:

> ... build and set up ... one bay of new building for lodging containing in length 18 foot and in breadth 18 foot.[43]

More generally, these covenants may indicate what access the tenant can have to the landlord's timber or stone, what repairs or redecoration must be undertaken (especially in later documents) and sometimes allow part of the building to be demolished without penalty.

Leases and conveyances occasionally include schedules of fittings either to be retained or to be included in the sale, which can be very informative. Thus, a 1793 lease of a house in Dead Lane, Coventry included a schedule of fittings, showing that the house (in a relatively low status area) was equipped with remarkable sophistication (Fig. 7.4). A deed for the sale of a mercer's house in the same city in 1660 gives a schedule of the shop fittings that were to be part of the sale, essentially listing all the items that, as fixtures, would be omitted from a probate inventory. They include:

> All the benches and forms there about the shopp … nine draw boxes behinde the doore going into the entry … one faire wainscote presse; seaven nests of large boxes … one paire of hopp scales and beame; one pair of sope scales … one wooden beame and scales with iron chaines … two leaden weights.[44]

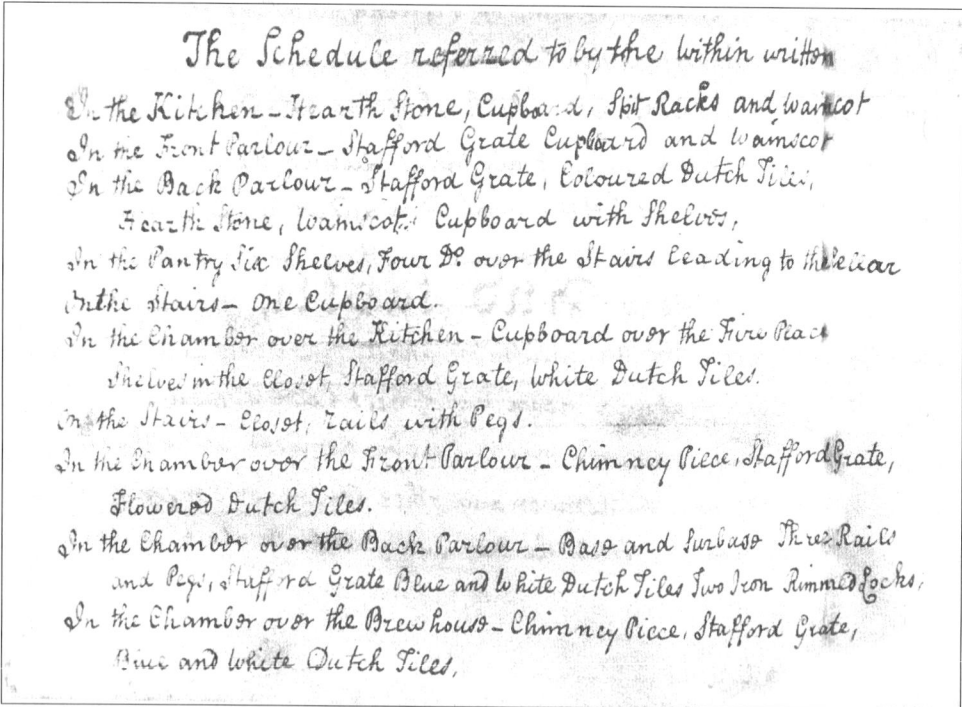

Fig. 7.4: Part of a schedule of fixtures in a lease of 1793 for a house in Dead Lane, Coventry
(Birmingham City Archives MS3117/1913-005/240861)

Newspapers

From the eighteenth century onwards, advertisements in local newspapers provide evidence both of building craftsmen and of trends in house styles. They regularly list the rooms in properties being offered for sale or rent (Fig. 7.5)

Personal documents and literary sources

Diaries and letters often give information about building work in progress or observed on visits, but they are rarely detailed enough to throw light on the decisions underlying the building process. One notable exception is found among the archives of Sir John Coke (1563-1644) who provided detailed notes for the builders working at his house in Derbyshire while he was involved on business in London. These instructions reveal much about his attitude to building, windows to be 'answerable in all proportions to the other two', precise placing of chimneys, etc.[45]

On MONDAY next, the 3d of JANUARY, 1820, at the SWAN INN, HENLEY-IN-ARDEN, in the County of Warwick, unless previously owned and the expences paid;

A Brown Mare, about Fourteen Hands high, appears to be rather broken of her Wind, and a Brown Pony, about Eleven Hands high, both of them taken up at MAPPLEBOROUGH GREEN, in the Parish of STUDLEY, in the said County, on the 7th of November last.

☞ To view the said Horses apply to WILLIAM GOODALL, Gamekeeper of Moreton Baggott, near Studley aforesaid.

To be Sold by Private Contract,

ALL that commodious, substantial, and modern-built Brick and Slate HOUSE and OFFICES, consisting of Three large dry Cellars, Two roomy Parlours with large Sash Windows, and spacious Entrance Hall in the centre, Two Chambers, and Attics of the same Size over Ditto, a Sitting Room, Kitchen, Pantry, and Dairy; Two Chambers, Store Room, Laundry, and Four Attics over the same; Brewhouse and Scullery detached; Coach-house, Store Room, Three-stall Stable, with Loft over Ditto; Coal-house, Granary, Pigeon and Poultry Houses; Piggeries, Yard, and Garden planted with choice Fruits, situated in the CASTLE END, in KENILWORTH aforesaid, and now in the Occupation of Mr. STREL, the Proprietor, who will give Immediate Possession thereof.

. These Premises are in excellent Repair, desirably situated within Four Miles of Leamington Spa, Five from Warwick, and Five from Coventry, between which Places the Roads are excellent, and Coaches pass and repass Eight times Daily.—The Purchaser of the above, may be accommodated with from Four to Eight Acres of Grass Land, to Rent, if required.

☞ To View the same, apply to Mr. BURSELL, King's Arms, Kenilworth; and for any further Particulars, to Mr. STEEL, of Kenilworth.

CRECY

WILL COVER this Season, at TALTON, Six Miles from Stratford-on-Avon, and Five from Shipston-on-Stower, at TEN GUINEAS and a CROWN thorough-bred Mares, all other Mares at FIVE GUINEAS and a Crown.

He was got by Walton, dam Cressida, by Old Whiskey, out of Young Giantess, by Diomed, (the Dam of Sorcerer and Eleanor.)

Good Accommodation for Mares and Foals at the usual price, and every attention will be paid to them.—All demands must be paid before the Mares are taken away.

NORWICH

Fig. 7.5: Advertisement for a house to be sold in Kenilworth, Warwickshire, from the *Warwick Advertiser* for January 1st 1820.

Poetry and novels have been little used as documents for housing, though they can catch the feeling of life in past societies in a way that is hidden in the factual information of inventories or building accounts. We can contrast two sixteenth century verses, Stephen Hawes ideal house

> Thus at the last I came into an halle
> Hanged with aras ryche and precyous
> And euery wyndowe glased with crystalle
>
> …
>
> The rofe dyde hange ryght hygh and pleasuntly
> By geometry made ryght well and craftely (1509).[46]

And the better known description of a Holderness cottage

> Of one bayes breadth, God wot, a silly cote,
> Whose thatched spars are furr'd with sluttish sotte
> A whole inch thick; shining like Blackmoors brows
> Through smok that down the headles barrel blows.
> At his beds-feete feeden his stalled teme
> His swine beneath, his pullen ore the beam (1597).[47]

These encapsulate the differing contemporary responses to grand and humble dwellings. Other obvious sources that can add to such pictures include the novels of Jane Austen and Charles Dickens.

The Builder

This weekly journal, published between 1842 and 1966, is a useful source of information for individual buildings (mainly larger houses and institutional buildings) though, as it lacks comprehensive indexes, the building date needs to be known approximately. Scanning its pages also reveals changes in design fashion. The first ten volumes (1842-1852) are available on-line (*http://www.bodley.ox.ac.uk/ilej/*).

Other sources

Many other types of document can contribute useful evidence. The vulnerability of timber-framed buildings led to numbers of towns suffering destructive fires, most notably, of course, the Great Fire of London. Following the fire, a Fire Court was established, whose decrees have been published, principally concerned with establishing ownership and when necessary arbitrating between rival claimants.[48] It is unclear if much evidence has been preserved of the London buildings destroyed by the fire, but other towns are better provided for. The court established after the fire of Warwick in 1694 dealt with ownership questions, but it also received claims of losses and disbursed the funds collected for those affected. The extensive records from this court have been published and include schedules of both the buildings destroyed and the losses of possessions.[49]

By the nineteenth century, social concern for the inadequacies of the housing available to the poor led to a number of Parliamentary Reports, which are very informative on housing standards. Those by Chadwick in 1841-2 and the Royal Commission in 1884-5 include particularly telling evidence.[50]

Many other sources, sometimes unexpected, can throw light on houses and building. A bundle of documents in a solicitor's collection proved to relate to the bankruptcy of a builder from Leamington Spa, Warwickshire, and to include detailed accounts for finishing the fitting out of a house he was working on when he became bankrupt, and also aggrieved letters from a prospective purchaser about the failure to complete the work.[51]

Medieval Housing

Although some types of records provide considerable evidence for housing in the medieval period, at best they include building evidence mixed in with much other material. Furthermore, most of the systematic sources relate to buildings of the status of manor houses or above, and their associated barns and out-buildings. For these, construction and repair costs are regularly included in manorial accounts.[52] Very rarely, the lord of the manor undertook repairs or the rebuilding of peasant houses, presumably to make the holding acceptable for a tenant; the cost would then be recorded in the manorial account rolls.[53]

Evidence for medieval village houses can be found systematically but sparsely in two sources, court rolls and coroner's inquests.

Manor Court Rolls

Court rolls record the admission of new copyhold tenants (Chapter 5) but the entries usually give little information about the property concerned beyond lists of fields or the size of holding and the presence of a messuage [house], barn, etc (Case Study 2). This generality has three exceptions. Before about 1600, when most copyhold tenure was similar to leasehold for life (or lives) rather than to freehold, the copyholders were responsible for the maintenance of their houses. The court jury regularly presented tenants for letting their houses get into disrepair, often requiring the repairs to be carried out before the next court. These presentments rarely describe the defects in detail but occasionally court papers include the jury's original detailed findings. Examples from Leek Wootton, Warwickshire and from the Durham Halmote court are particularly important for their indications of the use of cruck construction; the latter includes, for example, a house at Romanby, Northallerton, having three pair of *syles* (a dialect term for crucks) and two *endforkes*, which needed rebuilding.[54] A court roll of 1548 from Leek, Staffordshire gives a long list of timber required for repairs, in this case submitted by the tenants themselves, to assert their customary right to receive such timber. It includes a number of significant items, such as a tree needed for a chamber floor, another one to provide boards for a floor, and a pole for a ladder.[55] Other similar lists must remain to be noticed.

Admissions of tenants occasionally include an agreement to build or rebuild the house in lieu of an entry fine. These have been studied systematically for Worcestershire but do survive elsewhere.[56] They date predominantly from 1350 to 1500, reflecting the social dislocation following the Black Death, when some holdings were unoccupied for many years and their buildings became derelict. The Worcester agreements generally identify the size of the house in bays, its construction and materials. An admission showing modernisation at an unusually early date is found in Highhampton, Devon in 1519, when John Splott agreed to build 'unum caminum infra aulam dicti tenementi [a chimney within the hall of the said tenement]' within two years (cf Case Study 5).[57]

In the medieval period, houses were sometimes divided between family members, usually in the context of the retirement of an older person passing on their property in exchange for life-time rights to part of it; less commonly, such transactions took place between unrelated people, as part of a sale. The corresponding admission recorded in a manor court roll will often give details of the house; for example in 1419, William Notte, a widower, surrendered his tenement in Wymondham, Norfolk, to his son, reserving a room and solar at the north end of the hall, with permission to warm himself at the hall fire.[58]

Coroner's Inquests

These survive erratically but extensively from the mid-thirteenth century until c.1420; thereafter, the coroners ceased to be responsible to the Justices in Eyre and their rolls were no longer returned to London.[59] The rolls include inquests into deaths by violence and by misadventure (as well as some information on felonies, etc.). Perhaps half of the deaths by misadventure took place in the home and the details in the inquests can be very revealing of, for example, the strength of walls and doors, shared sleeping arrangements, the location of ovens in house yards, the stones around the open hearth supporting pots of boiling water.[60] A death in Warwick in 1390 gives an unusual insight into the character of houses – it was caused by the fall from a trestle of someone whitewashing and decorating a house.[61] These inquests are difficult to use but have been extensively analysed by Barbara Hanawalt in *The Ties that Bound*, (1986), concentrating on inquests for Northamptonshire and other counties in Eastern England. A selected series of national inquests is in print, as is the entire corpus for Bedfordshire.[62] It is noticeable that the specific examples are much more evocative of medieval lifestyles than are statistical analyses of the inquest evidence and of where violent deaths took place.

Individual documents

Many collections of medieval documents contain some giving details about houses. Like court rolls, deeds and leases may include building and partition agreements. As one example, an arbitration of 1448 for Fulwood, Warwickshire concerning dower rights gives a detailed picture of the manor house. Maud Fulwode, the widow, was assigned the use of the room over the hall in the manor of Fulwode until her son had made a chimney in the room beside the hall. She also had use of the parlour, the chapel, the kitchen, bakehouse and brewhouse, the garret over the gate, one of the barns and a byre and part of the garden.[63] For a village house, a lease of 1393 of a new-built house in Napton, Warwickshire, included a chamber and solar adjoining the upper end of the hall, together with an orchard and specified arable land.[64] Similar examples are encountered relatively frequently, but are very difficult to locate systematically.

Medieval building contracts have been collected and printed. They are very informative about building practices in that period, though rather less so about the layout of houses.[65] The 'drafts' that must have frequently been made to accompany such contracts have only very rarely survived, though one c. 1500 elevation of a timber-framed shop and house in Worcester is known.[66] Manorial surveys rarely include more than indications of the character of the manor house. However, a survey of the building defects in the church and rectory of Clifton Campville, Staffordshire in 1453 lists what appears to be every room in a large courtyard house. Notably, its parlour had a defective chimney, and the hall a 'ruined' louvre, while the 'Withdraghts' that accompanied the chambers had glazed windows.[67]

Wills sometimes include items relating to the home. Thus, for example, the 1562 will of William Waren of Fletchamstead, Warwickshire stated, 'I will that a chymne be made', while that of Thomas Addyngton of London in 1543 contained a surprisingly generous bequest, 'I will that a baye wyndowe be sett onto in the chambr of my neybur Maister Ilde at my proper costes and chardges'.[68]

[1]   See, for example, Eric Mercer, *English Vernacular Houses* HMSO, 1975, Matthew Johnson, *Housing Culture*, UCL Press, 1993 and Jane Grenville, *Medieval Housing,* Leicester University Press, 1997.

[2]   A C Edwards and K C Newton, *The Walkers of Hanningfield*, Buckland Publications, 1984. See also P Ryan, 'The buildings of rural Ingatestone, Essex, 1556-1601: 'Great Rebuilding' or 'Housing revolution'?', *Vernacular Architecture*, **31** (2000), 11.

[3]   K Hutton, 'The distribution of wheelhouses in the British Isles', *Agricultural History Review*, **24**(1) (1976), 30.

[4]   N W Alcock, 'Further houses-and-estate surveys', *Vernacular Architecture*, **5** (1974), 27; see also N W Alcock, 'Detailed house by house surveys', *Vernacular Architecture*, **1** (1970), 12.

[5]   Devon RO, 1508M/London – Estate Vals./4.

[6]   Somerset RO, DD/WO Box 43.

[7]   Blake Tyson, 'Twenty cruck buildings at Skelsmergh, Kendal, c. 1600', *Trans. Cumberland & Westmorland Antiquarian & Archaeol. Soc.*, 100 (2000), 181-206.

[8]   P Ryan, 'Ingatestone'

[9]   N W Alcock, 'Timber-framed buildings in north Bedfordshire. II. Post-medieval houses in Eaton Socon and Thurleigh', *Bedfordshire Archaeol J,* **4** (1969), 46.

[10]   N W Alcock & C Carson, *Houses Farms and Estates,* forthcoming.

[11]   M Spufford, 'The scope of local history and the potential of the Hearth Tax returns', *Local Historian* **30** (4) (2000), 202-221

[12]   D Harrington, S Pearson and S Rose (eds.), *Kent Hearth Tax Assessment Lady Day 1664*, British Record Society, 2000.

[13]   These problems are discussed in the introductions to the BRS series volumes.

[14]   Spufford, 'Scope', pp. 212-218.

[15]   They include R Potts, *A calendar of Cornish Glebe terriers, 1673-1735*, Devon and Cornwall Record Soc., NS19 (1974) and partial series for Berkshire, Buckinghamshire, Shropshire and Warwickshire.

[16]   Information from Brian Giggins.

[17]   A notable example is the c. 1600 terrier for High Bickington, Devon (DRO) which gives a detailed sketch plan of a large courtyard house with all its components labelled.

[18]   Devon RO, Glebe Terriers, Clyst St Mary.

[19]   See M W Barley, *The English Farmhouse and Cottage*, Routledge, 1961 for a wide-ranging discussion of their evidence.

[20]   Documents relating to Queen Anne's Bounty may be found in Diocesan ROs and at the Church of England Record Centre, Bermondsey. A good summary of the development of a vicarage documented from terriers and from the building itself is given by Sylvia Colman, 'Eye Vicarage: the documentation of a parsonage house, *Proc. Suffolk Inst. Archaeol.*, 34(1) (1977), 49-58.

[21]   For their location, see A J Camp, *Wills and their Whereabouts*, the author, 1974.

[22]   J and N Cox 'Probate inventories: the legal background', Part I, *Local Historian*, 16/2 (1984), 133-145; Part II, 16/4 (1984), pp. 217-228. See also J and N Cox, 'Valuations in probate inventories', Part I, *Local Historian*, 16/8 (1985), 467-478; Part II, 17/2 (1986), 85-100; J and N Cox, 'Probate, 1500-1800: a system in transition', in T Arkell, N Evans and N Goose (eds), *When Death do us part: Understanding and Interpreting the Probate Records of Early Modern England*, Leopards Head Press, 2000, pp. 14-37.

[23]   See Anne Tarver, *Church Court Records*, Phillimore 1995,

[24]   It is worth remembering that not all inventories can be expected to list rooms; they will not normally be given, for example, in inventories of lodgers or elderly 'retired' members of a

household. Such inventories can usually be recognised from their distinctive contents (see Alcock, *People at Home*, Phillimore, 1993, chapter 9). Some of the problems of matching the rooms in an inventory to a known house are considered above.

25 Alcock, *People at Home*, p. 200.

26 Lichfield Joint Record Office, 1617, Benett Shuckburgh

27 See the National Register of Archives, 'Corporate Name Detailed Search' (online at *http://www.hmc.gov.uk/business/busarchives.htm*) under 'Building and Construction/Builders'. A significant recent deposit at the London Metropolitan Archives comprises the archives of Reader Brothers, builders in East London

28 D Fry, 'Binley Woods: a Warwickshire example of Inter-war 'Shack and Track' development', *Warwickshire History*, 10(6) (1998/9), 191-202.

29 WCRO CR2433/31 (Margetts, Warwick); Buckinghamshire RO D/WIG/2/1/ (Wigley and Sons, Winslow; 115 volumes, 1875-1951); Gloucestershire RO D2080 (Moore and Sons, Tewkesbury; 3,000 notebooks, 1800-1925) East Sussex RO Acc. 6345 (A Burtenshaw and son, Hailsham), Accs. 768, 2600, 5529 (Vidler & Co., Rye).

30 N W Alcock, 'An Essex account for a building with ground-set posts in 1743', *Vernacular Architecture*, 31 (2000), 84.

31 Ipswich Borough Assembly Book, pp. 269-270, Suffolk RO C4/7/3/1. The placing of the parlour rather than the hall in the centre is surprising, going against the conventional interpretation of such lobby-entry plans in terms of privacy and access. I thank the now unknown correspondent who sent me this information many years ago.

32 University of Kansas, Kenneth Spencer Library, MS. Moore.

33 N W Alcock, 'Warwickshire Timber-framed houses: a draft and a contract', *Post-medieval Archaeol.*, **9** (1975), 213.

34 Both these drawings are from the important Bright family archive relating in part to estates in Herefordshire, which has migrated with its owners to Australia. See K.Morgan, 'The Bright family papers', *Archives*, 22 (1997), 119-129.

35 PRO C108/20 and C113/259; the drawings from the latter have now been transferred to MPA1/13/7-11.

36 They are reproduced fully in J Schofield (ed.), *The London Surveys of Ralph Treswell*, London Topographical Society, 135, 1987.

37 For locations, see M W Barley, *A guide to British topographical collections,* Council for British Archaeology, 1974.

38 Mary Dormer Harris, *A selection from the pencil drawings of Dr. Nathaniel Troughton,* Batsford, 1909.

39 A tradition of interior views developed earlier in Scotland, perhaps in response to the contrasts between the simplicity of Highland life and the sophistication of Edinburgh. See, for example, the pictures of David Wilkie.

40 Christiana Payne, *Rustic Simplicity: Scenes of Cottage Life in Nineteenth-century British Art,* University of Nottingham, 1998.

41 See, for example, Diana Sperling (1791-1862) *Mrs Hurst dancing and other scenes from Regency life 1812-1823* Gollancz, 1981; Caroline Davidson, *The world of Mary Ellen Best*, Chatto and Windus, 1985.

42 K T Ward, 'Covenants in conveying instruments: A note for the vernacular architectural historian', *Vernacular Architecture*, 25 (1994), 16-19.

43 Ibid. 17, quoting Bedfordshire RO, L. Jeayes, 533.

44 Selections only; the schedule is transcribed in Nat Alcock, 'Documentary records' in M. Rylatt and M A Stokes, *The Excavations at Broadgate East, Coventry, 1974-5*, Coventry Museums Monograph No. 5, 1996; the original deed is in Coventry City Archives, CCA/2/3/187.

45 See N Cooper, *Houses of the Gentry, 1480-1680*, Yale University Press, 1999, pp. 45, 215f.

46 Stephen Hawes, *The Pastime of Pleasure*, Early English Text Society, 1928, l. 2556f.

47 Bishop Joseph Hall, *Virdigemiarum, Lib. 5, Satire 1*, 1597, l. 58f. (Early English books 1475-1640, microfilm 320:9)

48 P E Jones, *The Fire Court*, 2 vols, Clowes, 1966.

49 M W Farr, *The Great Fire of Warwick, 1694*, Dugdale Society, **36**, 1992.

50 M W Flynn (ed.), *Report on the Sanitary Conditions of the Labouring Poor, (1842)* by Edwin Chadwick, Edinburgh University Press, 1965; *Royal Commission for inquiring into the Housing of the Working Classes*, First Report with Minutes of Evidence, 1884-5, Cmnd 4402. These are widely available through the microfilm series of Parliamentary Papers.

51 N W Alcock, 'The building of Clarendon Crescent, Leamington Spa, 1830-1840', *Warwickshire History*, 10(6) (1998/9), 213-229.

52 See, for example, the evidence collected in R Allen Brown, H M Colvin and A J Taylor, *The History of the King's Works, Vols. I-II: The Middle Ages*, H.M.S.O., 1963.

53 E.g. N W Alcock, 'The medieval cottages at Bishop's Clyst, Devon', *Medieval Archaeology*, **9** (1965), 146.

54 See N W Alcock and R de Z Hall, 'Documentary evidence for crucks' in N . Alcock (ed.), *Cruck Construction: an Introduction and Catalogue*, Council for British Archaeology, 1981, p. 34.

55 PRO SC2/202/65. I thank Dr Faith Cleverdon for this reference.

56 R K Field, 'Worcestershire peasant building in the later Middle Ages', *Medieval Archaeology*, **9** (1965), 105.

57 Devon RO, CR552.

58 See N W Alcock, 'The Medieval Peasant at Home: England, 1250-1550' in C Beattie, A Maslakovic and S R Jones (eds), *The Medieval Household in Christian Europe*, University of York, 2003, citing Elaine Clark, 'Some Aspects of Social Security in Medieval England', *J. Family History*, 7 (1982), 318. In the post-medieval period, a husband sometimes bequeathed such rights to his widow (Case study 4).

59 PRO JUST2.

60 For these examples, see Alcock, 'Medieval Peasant'.

61 PRO JUST2/188, m.1, no. 2.

62 C S Gross (ed.) *Select Cases from the Coroners' Rolls: 1265-1413*, Selden Society, 9 (1896); R F Hunnisett (ed.), *Bedfordshire Coroners' Rolls*, Bedfordshire Historical Record Society, 41 (1961). See also, R F Hunnisett(ed.) *Sussex Coroners' Inquests: 1485-1558*, Sussex Record Society, 74 (1984-5).

63 SBTRO DR37/1/949

64 WCRO CR1248/71/23.

65 L F Salzman, *Building in England down to 1540*, Oxford, 1967.

66 F W B Charles and K Down, 'A sixteenth century drawing of a timber-framed town house', *Trans. Worcestershire Archaeol. Soc.*, 3rd Ser. 3 (1970-2), 67-78.

67 R Hutchinson and N J Tringham, 'A medieval rectory house at Clifton Campville, Staffordshire', *South Staffordshire Archaeol. Hist. Soc. Trans.* 32 (1990-1), 83-84.

68 Lichfield Joint Record Office, 1562, William Waren; Kenneth Spencer Library, University of Kansas, Hoffman-Freeman Collection, 31:126.

Fig. 8.1: Hines House, Clifford Chambers, Warwickshire (a) the front at the present day
(photo: N. W. Alcock) (b) the rear in about 1900 (WCRO CR2199/6/28).

8. Case Studies

These case studies do not present full histories of the houses concerned, but concentrate on different aspects in each study. Principally, they examine the sources of evidence used to establish the sequence of owners and tenants, dealing with title deeds in the first example, manorial court rolls in the second and Deed Registry entries in the third. The fourth shows how snippets of evidence can be assembled to solve a difficult problem and the final case study includes one approach to the interpretation of probate inventories and the understanding of life-styles.

1. History Through Title Deeds

Hines House, Clifford Chambers, Gloucestershire (now Warwickshire)

This former farmhouse stands on a very isolated site more than a mile from the village of Clifford Chambers.[1] The front of the house is of brick and the other three sides are rendered, but old photographs show that they are of timber-framing in a relatively late style (Fig. 8.1). Although the brick front might have been a casing for earlier framing, a close study of the structure showed that the timberwork fitted around the brickwork. Thus, the house was built using mixed brick and timber construction at a time when timber-framing was going out of use in the Midlands. A consideration of the style of both the brick and timber work suggested that it dated from about 1720.

The Warwickshire CRO index of maps pin-pointed a plan of 1807, showing the farm as part of the estate of one William Devaynes, mainly located in the adjoining parish of Atherstone-on-Stour, Warwickshire. This estate was known to have been bought by James West, owner of the near-by Alscot Park estate in 1844 (VCH and other sources); it was sold to the present owner's family in 1923. The West estate records in WCRO are only listed in outline, but it was possible to identify those relating to Atherstone and find the bundle relating to the 1844 purchase. This gave the history of Hines House from 1755 onwards.

In that year, John Bullock of Sharnbrook, Bedfordshire, bought the farm from Thomas Hiron of Alveston (a near-by village). It was then called Heath Farm, comprising 162 acres and formerly occupied by Thomas Holtham, then by William Hind (Hine or Hyne in other sources); thus, it was from this tenant that the farm was named.[2] Bullock had bought the Manor of Atherstone a few years earlier, and in 1796 his family sold the whole estate to William Devaynes. The handsome sale catalogue (Fig. 8.2) gives full details of the property – and identifies Devaynes as being of the 'East India Company', information it would have been very difficult to find elsewhere.

A clue to the earlier history of the farm came from a covenant in the 1755 sale deed. This guaranteed that in the purchase by Thomas Hiron (27-8 Sept 1749) of this and other property, the ownership should not be affected by any acts possibly done by

> 'Randolph Greenway, or Abel Makepeace and Martha his wife, both deceased, which Martha is the relict of Edward Clopton, Esquire, and daughter, heir and only child of John Combe, Esquire [*correctly of William Combe*]'.

Warwickſhire and Glouceſterſhire.

PARTICULARS

OF

A CAPITAL

FREEHOLD-ESTATE,

COMPRISING

THE MANOR OF ATHERSTONE,

WITH

ATHERSTONE, AILSTONE, AND HINES's FARMS,

CONTAINING TOGETHER

ONE THOUSAND AND THIRTY ACRES OF RICH

ARABLE, PASTURE *and* MEADOW LAND,

PART TYTHE FREE,

IN HIGH CULTIVATION,

DESIRABLY SITUATE

WITH THE RIVER-STOUR AND THE HIGH-ROAD FROM LONDON TO BIRMINGHAM,

RUNNING THROUGH THE ESTATE,

THREE MILES FROM STRATFORD-UPON-AVON,

IN THE COUNTIES OF WARWICK AND GLOUCESTER,

WITH

SUITABLE DWELLING-HOUSES,

BARNS AND OUTBUILDINGS,

SIXTEEN COTTAGES, GARDENS, &c.

LET TO

Mr. JOHN BOOT,

AT AN OLD RENT OF

SEVEN HUNDRED AND SIXTY POUNDS PER ANNUM;

WHICH WILL BE SOLD BY AUCTION,

By Mr. SMITH,

AT

GARRAWAY's COFFEE-HOUSE, 'CHANGE-ALLEY, CORNHILL,

On *THURSDAY,* the 14th of *APRIL,* 1796,

At TWELVE o'CLOCK,

(IN ONE LOT.)

May be viewed by applying to the Tenant, of whom PARTICULARS may be had; alſo at the *White-Hart, Chipping-Norton; Bear, Woodſtock; Warwick-Arms, Warwick; Hotel, Birmingham; King's-Head, Coventry; Star, Oxford,* at the *White-Lion,* and of Mr. WHEELER, Solicitor, *Stratford-upon-Avon;* and of Mr. *SMITH,* No. 62, *Broad-Street,* near the *Royal Exchange, London,* where a Plan of the ESTATE may be ſeen.

(3)

HINES's-FARM,

ADJOINING TO AILSTONE-FARM,

CONTAINS

ONE HUNDRED AND FIFTY-EIGHT ACRES (BE THE SAME MORE OR LESS) OF RICH PASTURE LAND, TYTHE FREE,

WITH

A FARM-HOUSE, OXHOUSE, BARN, STABLING, AND OUTBUILDINGS,

Let on Leafe, with ATHERSTONE and AILSTONE FARMS, to Mr. JOHN BOOT, a refponfible Tenant, for a Term, of which Eighteen Years will be unexpired at *Michaelmas*, 1796,

At an *old* Rent of SEVEN HUNDRED and SIXTY POUNDS *per Annum*; Land-Tax allowed, about 2s. in the Pound.

THE MANOR

Abounds with GAME, *and commands a* SITUATION *juftly efteemed for its Beauties, Richnefs of Soil, and genteel Neighbourhood, through which the* RIVER-STOUR *runs for a confiderable Diftance, annexing a valuable* FISHERY *to the Property.—Diftance from* BIRMINGHAM *Twenty Miles,* AULCESTER *Eight, Eight from* WARWICK, *Ninety-one Miles from* LONDON, *and Three from* STRAT-FORD-UPON-AVON, *in the* COUNTIES *of* WARWICK *and* GLOUCESTER.

The TIMBER is to be taken by the Purchafer down to One Shilling *per* Stick.

CONDITIONS OF SALE.

I. THE higheft Bidder to be the Purchafer, and if any Difpute arife, the ESTATE to be put up again.

II. No Perfon to advance lefs than FIFTY POUNDS at each Bidding.

III. The Purchafer to pay down immediately a Depofit of TWENTY *per* Cent. in Part of the Purchafe-Money, and fign an Agreement for Payment of the Remainder, on or before the 25th of *June*, 1796, on having a good Title.

IV. The Purchafer fhall have proper Conveyances of the ESTATE, (at his own Expence) on Payment of the Remainder of the Purchafe-Money, agreeable to the Third Condition; and all Out-goings fhall be cleared up to *Midfummer*, 1796, from which Time the Purchafer will be entitled to the Rents and Profits arifing from the ESTATE.

V. There being a Duty on all Sales of Eftates, &c. of 3½d. in the Pound, the ESTATE comprifed in this Particular is to be fold fubject to the Seller paying one Moiety of the faid Tax, and the Buyer the other, exclufive of the Sum the faid ESTATE fhall fell for.

Laftly, If the Purchafer fhall neglect or fail to comply with the above Conditions, the Depofit-Money to be forfeited, and the Proprietor fhall be at full Liberty to re-fell the faid ESTATE; and the Deficiency by fuch fecond Sale, together with all Charges attending the fame, to be made good by the Defaulter at this prefent Sale.

The above Estates sold to — Devaynes & East & die Company for 90,300£ *The*

Fig. 8.2: Section of a 1796 sale catalogue for a Gloucestershire estate, of which Hines Farm (the later Hines House), Clifford Chambers was part (SBTRO ER6/7).

Both the Clopton and Combe families were prominent in Stratford-upon-Avon and numerous records relating to them survive, including several references to property in Clifford Chambers. Sorting these out in order revealed the following sequence of events. A settlement in 1667 by William Combe included

> Inclosed grounds called, the Rye Piece, one Furze Ground called Oxleys, three closes or Furzen Grounds called the Heaths, one close or meadow lying between the Shepherd's house and Ayleston Fields [*in Atherstone-on-Stour*], all in Clifford Chambers.

This was inherited by William's only child, Martha, and the settlement on her second marriage to Abel Makepeace in 1731 included a messuage called Heath Farm and lands in Clifford Chambers, occupied by Richard Spiers. These were to revert to the Clopton family after the deaths of Abel and Martha. In 1738, Edward Clopton (Martha's son) sold it to Randolph Greenway, by which time the tenant was Thomas Holtham. No documents survive for the 1749 sale to Thomas Hiron, but it is referred to in the 1755 deed.[3]

The very first reference to what was to become the farm is in 1649 when Henry Rainsford, lord of the manor of Clifford Chambers, was in great financial difficulties (see also p. 88). In that year, he sold all his property in Ailston (straddling the parish boundary between Clifford Chambers and Atherstone-on-Stour) to one Jonas Godschalk, excluding from this sale land which would otherwise have been part of Ailston

'five pieces of land called The Heathes, containing 150 acres', in Clifford Chambers. This exclusion was almost certainly required because he had already sold the land to the Combe family.[4]

Thus, the deeds document the origin of Hines Farm as a series of fields enclosed from heathland (probably in the early seventeenth century) and used for about a century as rough pasture. In about 1720, the present farmhouse was built there, which presumably superseded the 'Shepherd's House' mentioned in 1667 (on a different site). Later information is relatively sparse. Hines Farm was being leased as part of the large Atherstone Farm from about 1800 and by the time of the 1851 census was being occupied by a family of farm labourers. Fortunately, the enumerator's books from 1851 to 1891 identified Hines Farm (or Hines Cottage) by name, so the families living there can be recognised. From 1871 onwards, it was divided into two cottages.

The history of Hines House is summarised in Table 8.1

---

1   Clifford Chambers is very close to Stratford-upon-Avon, but was in Gloucestershire until 1931. Although some administrative records for the parish, such as the Land Tax assessments, are in Gloucestershire RO, most of the archives relating to the village are in either the Warwickshire CRO(WCRO) or the Shakespeare Birthplace Trust RO (SBTRO), Stratford-upon-Avon. The house was formerly known as Hines Farm.

2   The 1752 will of Thomas Holtham (Gloucestershire RO) names his daughter Mary Hyne, and the parish register for Ilmington, Warwickshire includes the marriage in 1733 of Mary Holtham and William Hinde. Thus, the change of tenant kept the farm in the same family.

3   1667, WCRO L6/217; 1731, SBTRO ER3/2894-5; 1738, SBTRO ER3/2897-8.

4   British Library Add. Ch. 42988.

Table 8.1   Ownership summary for Hines House

Date	Event
c. 1649	'The Heathes' sold by lord of the manor of Clifford Chambers to Thomas Combe
1667	Included in family settlement by William Combe
c. 1720	The house is built
1731	Martha Clopton (formerly Combe) marries Abel Makepeace
1738	Edward Clopton sells the farm to Randolph Greenway; tenant Thomas Holtham
1749	Sold to Thomas Hiron
1755	Sold to John Bullock; tenant William Hind/Hine
1796	Sold to William Devaynes
1844	Sold to James West
From 1840s	Occupied as farm labourer's cottages
1923	Sold to present owner's family and becomes a family home

2. A Medieval Copyhold Farm

Cuttle Pool Farm, Knowle, Warwickshire

This house history started with the building itself, a late-medieval timber-framed house of very heavy construction which had been tree-ring dated to 1479; it was extended and cased in brick at the end of the eighteenth century (Fig. 8.3).[1] It stands near a former mill pool drained in the eighteenth century, the Cuttle Pool from which it was named. The owner's title deeds went back to 1904, when the farm was bought from the local

Fig. 8.3: Cuttle Pool Farm, Knowle, Warwickshire. The eighteenth-century brick walling replaces the exterior framing of a late medieval timber-framed house, which is otherwise almost intact (photo: N W Alcock).

Springfield Hall estate. The deeds for the estate showed that Cuttle Pool Farm (then only 60 acres) had been bought in 1849 from the Manor of Knowle estate. Earlier deeds relating to the manor seem not to have survived, but a map and survey of 1816 showed the layout of the farm and gave the occupant as Sarah Chinn. The survival of the map and these deeds was fortunate, since the 1910 'Domesday' records for Knowle are lost (both the Field and Valuation books) and post-1832 Land Tax records do not survive either. A search of the WCRO indexes for Knowle produced one stray lease for the farm, dated 25th March 1747. In this, William Smith, the lord of the manor, leased the farm to one Thomas Chinn, yeoman, whose family were to continue as tenants there for more than 150 years.[2]

The 1747 lease also stated that the farm had recently been bought from John Evetts, implying that it was a freeholding within the manor of Knowle; unless earlier deeds could be found, it seemed likely that its earlier history would be difficult to establish. However, a 1605 survey of the manor of Knowle suggests a different status for the farm. It includes a property which comprised (in abstract)

> two messuages and one house next to Cuttle Pool with a dwelling house of four bays and a total of 50 acres land, which was held by Robert Wilcox at a rent of 18s 3d by a copy of court roll granted on 12th July 1591, the former tenants being Laurence and Nicholas Ebrall.

A later survey (1635) gave a similar but simpler description of 'two messuages near Cuttlepoole', again with a rent of 18s 3d; the tenants were Ann Catesby and John Catesby (probably her son).[3]

Numerous court rolls survive for the manor of Knowle and it seemed worthwhile to search for later references, possibly including admissions to the holding or the enfranchisement (conversion to freehold) of the copyholding.[4] The admission of John Catesby (the father), Ann and John (the son) in 1608 soon came to light, and they also appeared in rentals at this period. A 1648 roll referred to land 'late in the tenure of John Catesby', but a break in the series of rolls left his successor as tenant uncertain. However, the admission in 1691 of William and Elizabeth Evetts to property to be held to the use of William and Elizabeth and their heirs (i.e. as a marriage settlement) referred to the 1689 surrender by William Evetts. The property then comprised a messuage, barns, etc and 'le Backside known as Cuttlepoole house' and various named fields (but not the whole of the farm, as William's mother held some of it in dower).

Presumably, William's father, Laurence Evetts (who must have died in about 1688) had succeeded John Catesby some time before 1648; in a 1649 court he was required to scour a ditch between Cuttle Mill Green and 'his ground', suggesting that he had taken over by then. In the 1666 Hearth Tax, he had one of the largest assessments in Knowle, with four hearths, identifying him as one of the most comfortably-off people in the community.[5]

Another gap in the sequence of rolls from 1712 to 1727 probably includes the presentment of the death of William Evetts and the admission of his son John; an entry in the 1728 roll relating to other property describes it as 'adjoining the land formerly of William Evetts, deceased' and (later in the entry) as 'adjoining the land of John Evetts'. Searching through the later rolls located various references to the Evetts family, but two were of crucial importance. In 1735 John mortgaged the farm to one John Weetman of Baddesley Clinton, and the roll records a 'conditional surrender', to be void if he repaid the £640 to Weetman. Finally, in 1746, John Weetman and John Evetts in consideration of £860 (the total purchase price) surrendered the property to trustees for William Smith, the lord of the manor of Knowle. With this transaction, the eighteenth century ownership sequence was complete.[6]

Working back from 1605 in the court rolls proved less difficult, despite a large gap in the series. The admission on 12th July 1591 (referred to in the 1605 survey) proved to be the surrender by Laurence and Nicholas Ebrall in favour of Robert Wilcockes; another admission in 1607 of Thomas Ebrall, the son of Nicholas, may have established a claim to the property that John Catesby (admitted two years earlier) had to buy out; fortunately, this entry gave the admission date for Nicholas Ebrall (15th April 1583) and named the previous tenant, Robert Branthurst, which was valuable as the 1583 roll is lost. A gap in the rolls from 1544 to 1578 could be bridged using a survey of 1540, which listed William Barnethurst holding by copy of court roll dated 6th July 1534

'A messuage and ... two cottages ... lying beside Cotyll Mill ...', still paying 18s 3d rent.[7]

This clearly relates to the property described in the 1605 survey and we can presume that William Barnethurst (or Branthurst) was succeeded by Robert between 1544 and 1578, and the latter by Laurence and Nicholas Ebrall in 1583.

The 1534 roll does survive and shows William's admission following the death of his father, Thomas, whose own copy was dated 1521; this roll also exists and records the surrender of the property by Robert Richardes and the admission of Thomas Branthurst, whose wife Alice (by then dead) was Robert's daughter – presumably his only child (Fig. 8.4). The farm was to be held by Robert until his death and then by Thomas and his heirs. Thomas may well have been living at Cuttle Pool with his father-in-law and helping him with the farm. In 1525, the death of Robert was reported to the court, but no new admission was needed.

The 1521 roll recorded Robert's own admission in 1475 but that year's roll is lost. However, since the house was built in or soon after 1479, he was clearly its original occupier and he must have commissioned its building. His direct descendants continued to live there until 1583.

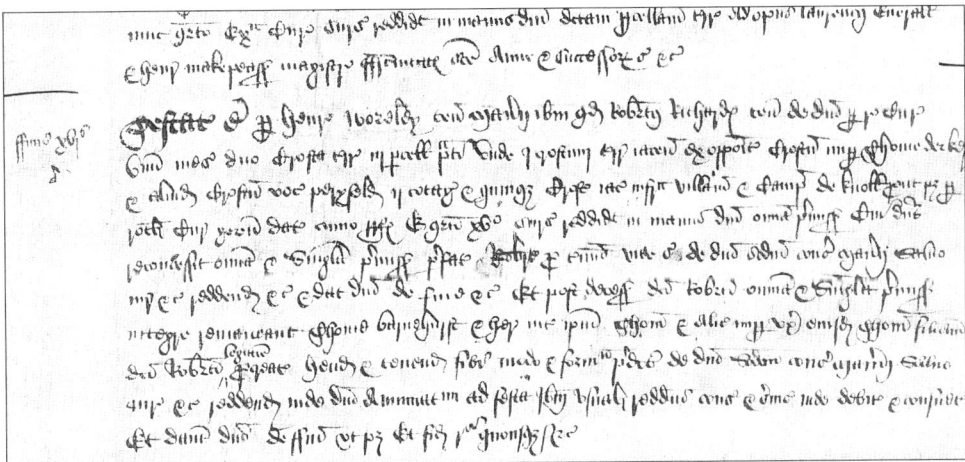

Fig. 8.4: Manor court entry for Cuttle Pool Farm in 1521, surrender by Robert Richardes and admission of Thomas Barnethurst (WCRO CR1886/315).

One puzzle remains, the description in the court rolls as 'two messuages and five cottages'. As this recurs more or less unchanged back to the earliest record in 1521 (and by implication in 1475), Cuttle Pool Farm must be the sole survivor of a hamlet, which existed at some time before 1475. Clearly, the two main properties (the messuages) had been combined and rebuilt as one house, while the cottages had been abandoned and their land added to the farm. Without further evidence, the date at which the hamlet disappeared cannot be established but this could have taken place well before 1475 and a post-Black Death desertion is plausible.

The history of Cuttle Pool Farm is summarised in Table 8.2

Table 8.2 Ownership summary for Cuttle Pool Farm

Date	Event
1475	Robert Richardes admitted to hold the farm by copyhold
c. 1479	He rebuilds the house
1521	Thomas Barnethurst, son-in-law of Robert Richardes admitted; succeeds on Robert's death in 1525
1534	William Barnethurst succeeds on Thomas's death
before 1583	Robert Branthurst (or) Barnethurst succeeds William
1583	Laurence and Nicholas Ebrall admitted on surrender or death of Robert Branthurst
1591	Robert Wilcox admitted on surrender of Laurence and Nicholas Ebrall and their wives
1608	John Catesby, senior, Ann and John, junior, admitted on surrender of Robert Wilcox
c. 1648	Laurence Evetts succeeds John Catesby, junior, as copyholder
c. 1688	William Evetts succeeds his father Laurence
c. 1727	John Evetts succeeds his father William
1746	Sold by John Evetts to William Smith, lord of the manor of Knowle and owner of Knowle Hall; conversion from copyhold to freehold
1747	Lease to Thomas Chinn
1849	Sale to Springfield Hall estate by Knowle Hall estate (manor of Knowle)
1904	Sale by Springfield Hall estate. End of tenancy by Chinn family

---

[1] The year is that in which the trees were felled, and the traditional practice of using timber green means that we can be confident that the house was built either in that year or at most a year or two later. The house is described in N W Alcock, 'Smoke Bay or Open Hall? Cuttle Pool Farm, Knowle, Warwickshire', *Vernacular Architecture*, **29** (1998), 82-84.

[2] Springfield Hall deeds, WCRO CR1516; 1816 Knowle map and survey, WCRO CR982, CR2151/107; 1747 lease, WCRO CR1327.

[3] 1605, PRO LR2/228; 1635, Coventry RO PA309/149.

[4] WCRO CR1886 for 1472 to 1671; CR2151 for 1689 to 1934.

[5] WCRO Z336/1. He had six hearths in 1674, but is listed under a different village, so Cuttle Pool must have been leased.

[6] In principle, William Smith as lord of the manor, should have executed a deed of enfranchisement to convert the copyholding to freehold. However, as he was simultaneously the lord of the manor and the copyhold tenant of the property, he may not have thought this formality necessary.

[7] PRO LR2/185

3. A London Suburban House

9 Malvern Road, Hackney

London's nineteenth century growth led to the building of innumerable streets of new houses whose building history can be documented through the Middlesex Deeds Registry. This research relates to part of such a development, half of a semi-detached pair of houses, the central one of three such pairs (Fig. 8.5). In the nineteenth century, the area was regarded as part of the north London suburb of Dalston, though ecclesiastically it lies within the parish of St John, Hackney. The key questions for the research were:

When was the house built?
Who built it and who were its early occupants?

Fig. 8.5: Exterior of one of three adjoining semi-detached pairs of houses, nos. 5,7; 9, 11 and 13, 15 Malvern Road, Hackney (photo: N W Alcock).

Map evidence indicates an approximate building date. The house must have been built between 1842, when the site was still a field, used as a market garden (belonging to Thomas and William Rhodes)[1] and 1870, the date that the first large-scale Ordnance Survey map was surveyed. Within this period, the 1850s was suspected because a similar house in a near-by street had a datestone of 1854. The *Metropolitan Board of Works Renumbering and Renaming Notices* showed that the house must have existed before 1863. In that year, the former 4 Malvern Cottages was renumbered 9 Malvern Road. Previously, the road had contained several blocks of houses, each separately numbered (and probably each built as part of a separate project). Malvern Cottages consisted of one detached house followed by three semi-detached pairs (nos. 2-7).[2] The 1851 census listed the occupants of no 1 Malvern Cottages and showed the others as 'being built'. In 1861, the whole block was occupied.

The Hackney archivist was able to confirm that the area belonged to the Rhodes family, forming part of their Lamb Farm estate which was being developed at this period. An 1870s partition of the estate and the attached schedule gave some more information. The lease for the pair of houses 9 and 11 Malvern Road expired at Lady Day 1940 and the ground rent was £10 (but the starting date of the lease was not stated). The Hackney Archives held no deeds at all for Malvern Road itself, but one bundle for a house in a nearby street (3 Caroline Cottages, Albert Road) included the assignment in 1863 of an original agreement of 1854 made by Thomas and William Arthur Rhodes to one James Stanborough, builder, which must have been similar to that made for 4 Malvern Cottages.[3]

With this information, the obvious next step was a search in the Middlesex Registry of Deeds for this corresponding lease. The search was straightforward in principle: Use the index to locate deeds with the Rhodes as grantors and then check the memorials to find the right deed. The task proved rather onerous, as Thomas and William Arthur Rhodes made almost 90 grants in Hackney in the years 1850-1854, and they and other members of the family made at least as many elsewhere. The memorials for 1854 contained one Malvern Road deed and those for 1850 none at all, bracketing the relevant period; eventually, in the 1851 memorials, a series of leases to Richard Liscombe, builder, was located, including nos. 2-3, 4-5 and 6-7 Malvern Cottages. In each lease, the land on which a pair of houses had been built was leased for 89 years from 25th March 1851. All the leases were dated 24th July 1851, although they were registered at different dates. Each lease was followed by the memorial for a mortgage of the pair of houses for £200; 4-5 Malvern Cottages was mortgaged to Thomas Knight, oilman, of Newgate Street, London.[4] Entries for Liscombe as grantor in the index and for Knight to Liscombe then led to the deed for the redemption of the mortgage and to the sub-lease of no. 4 Malvern Cottages. The first took place on 18th May 1851, and ten days later (28th May), a lease was granted by Liscombe to Elizabeth Watson of 8 Forest Road, Dalston; the period was 87 1/4 years and the rent £6 per year.[5]

This was not quite the end of the story as seen in the deed registry. Following through the tenants year by year was most easily done through the street directories.[6] The first one covering Malvern Road (1854) showed the occupier of 4 Malvern Cottages as Henry Pritchard, esquire, rather than Elizabeth Watson, and he was still there in the 1860 directory. A return to the index for the deed registry found a reference to the assignment by Elizabeth Watson on 17th March 1853 of her lease, to Henry Pritchard, gentleman, then of 3 Richmond Villas, Dalton, followed by his mortgage to one Clement Uzielli of 23 Threadneedle Street, London.[7]

About to be leased to Mr Liscombe

44 3

About to be leased to Mr Liscombe

About to be leased to Mr Liscombe

Gardens

102 3

102 3

Houses

4 5

Fore Courts

44 3

Malvern Road

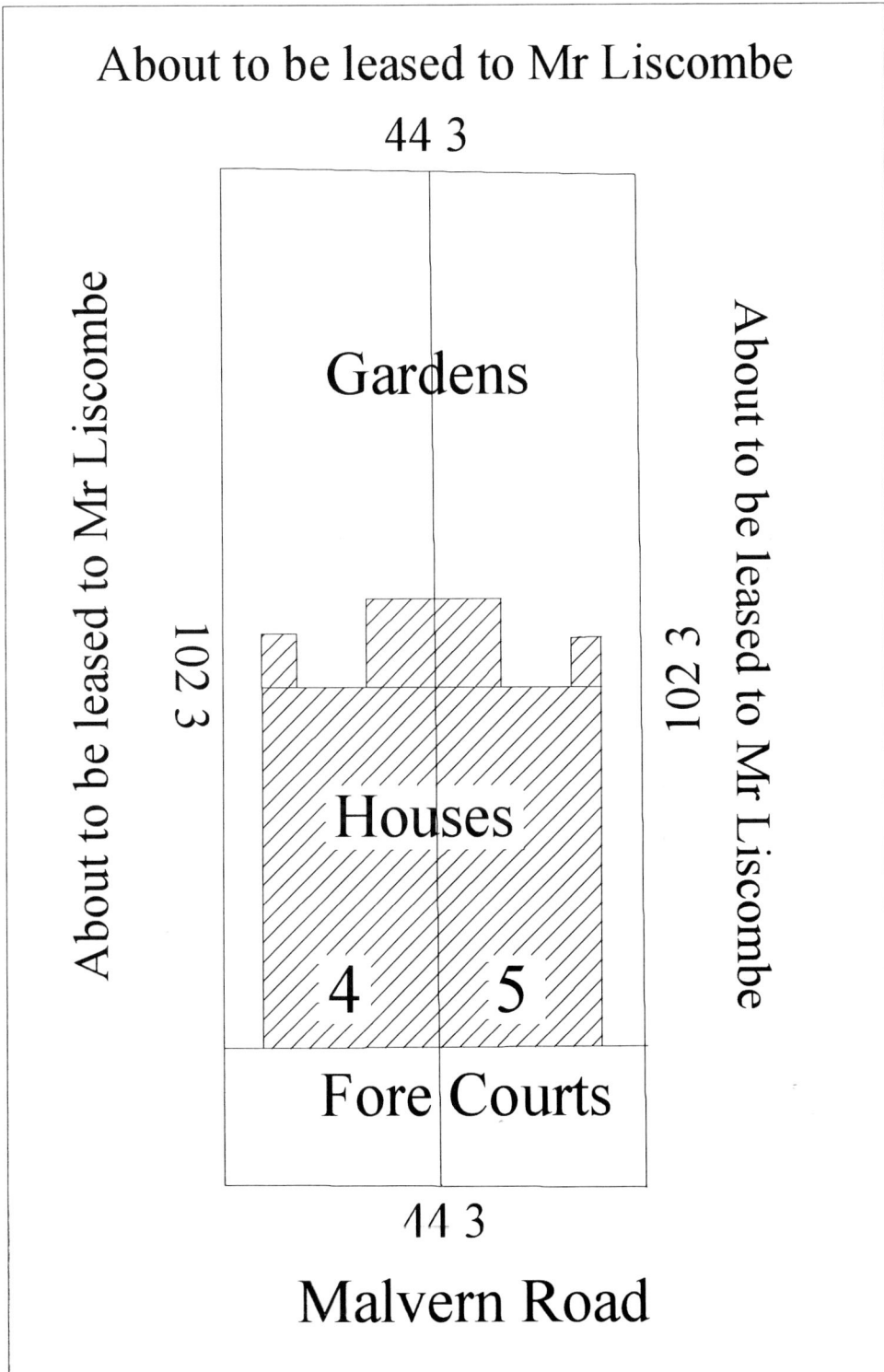

Fig. 8.6: Plot plan from Middlesex Registry of Deeds for 4-5 Malvern Cottages, Hackney (later 9, 11 Malvern Road) (redrawn from LMA MDR 1851/11, no. 58). Dimensions are in feet and inches.

Thus, the answer to the original questions was that the house must have been completed in early 1851 and was occupied by May in that year; the builder was Richard Liscombe and the occupier Elizabeth Watson. The actual building process is not made altogether clear by the memorials. Both the lease from Rhodes to Liscombe and that by him to Elizabeth Watson have plans showing the building plots *and* the houses on them (Fig. 8.6), and the latter, surprisingly is dated before the former.[8] The key to understanding the building of the house lies in the agreement that must have been made between the Rhodes brothers and Liscombe. Although this has not been preserved, we can infer something about it from the information in the leases and from a book of 'Lamb Farm Estate Rough Notes'. This includes memoranda of a series of Malvern Road agreements from 1853-5, where the rent was calculated at 2s 6d to 3s 6d per foot of frontage. Another item states that one year was to be at a peppercorn rent, and if not sold the next year's rent would also be a peppercorn. Finally, a slightly enigmatic note reads

£120 the debt at £20 each house

Bricks will come to £70 each house

Money to advance £100 each house.[9]

Putting all this together, we can infer that for the three pairs of houses, 2-7 Malvern Cottages, the initial agreement would have been made in about March 1850, with a total ground rent of £30 (3 x 44 ft frontage per pair). A cash payment was probably not also demanded, but one may have been required when the actual lease was signed.[10] The building would have taken place in the summer of 1850 for all six houses, with fitting out over the winter and occupation in 1851. The money to buy the bricks, etc. would come from the £200 mortgages taken out for each pair. These were almost certainly the subject of other agreements (which have not survived), one for each pair of houses; under these, the money would have been released in stages as work progressed. The mortgages were only formally executed a year later.[11] The houses were then sold, the lease assigned or a sub-lease made, and the mortgage paid off. The cost to the final purchasers is unknown, but 3 Caroline Cottages, Albert Road was mortgaged for £146 in 1863, suggesting a price of £180-200. This would have given Liscombe a respectable profit on his outlay. [12]

Some further details for the house have been filled in from census enumerations and directories. Henry Pritchard was identified as the head clerk to a firm of stationers in the 1861 census, but by 1865, he had been replace by John Burt who was dead by 1871, when his widow, a costume maker, was head of the household.[13] There seems to have been a rapid turnover of occupants in the following years (see Table 8.3). In 1891 and 1901, the census shows three separate households at No. 9, implying that the house had been split into flats.

For the twentieth century, the details are unclear, because after 1900 the directories only list trades-people, rather than all residents. The electoral register for 1901 lists Richard Broadley while that for 1921 has five qualified voters and for 1939 no less than eleven.[14] Frustratingly, it has not been possible to use the 1910 'Domesday' evidence, because the particular map sheet needed to identify the hereditament number is missing at the PRO.[15]

The later ownership and tenancy of the house is uncertain and a further unresolved question is what happened when the original lease (and the sub-lease) expired in 1940. The Middlesex Deeds Registry is not useful for this information, because it ceased to cover this part of north London when compulsory title registration was instituted in 1899. However, the Land Registry provided a copy of their register, which shows that the ownership was first recorded in 1926. Because the deed of that date included a restrictive covenant (which was listed in the register), the Registry provided a copy of the deed. It proved to be the sale by the Rhodes Estate to one Henry Austin of over one hundred of their ground rents, covering the whole of this section of Hackney; the deed includes a schedule listing details of all the original leases and presumably the counterpart leases were then handed over to the purchaser. Five years later, the freehold of No. 9 itself was sold on to one Abraham Goldstine, but details of later sales are not shown in the current property register and nor does it list further transfers of Liscombe's sub-lease.[16]

The history of 9 Malvern Road, Hackney is summarised in Table 8.3.

Table 8.3 Ownership summary for 9 Malvern Road, Hackney

Date	Event
1850	Agreement between Rhodes brothers and Richard Liscombe for building three pairs of houses and one single house
March 1851	Lease executed between Rhodes brothers and Liscombe Mortgage of 4-5 Malvern Cottages to Thomas Knight
May 1851	Liscombe's mortgage redeemed Sub-lease by Liscombe to Elizabeth Watson
1853	Assignment of lease by Elizabeth Watson to Henry Pritchard Mortgage by Pritchard to Clement Uzielli
1861	Henry Prichard, head clerk to stationers with his wife, two daughters, a boarder and a servant (1861 census)
1865-71	John Burt (directories); Mary Ann Burt, widow with four children, two boarders and a servant (1871 census)
1876	Thomas Stanley (directory)
1881-1901	1881: Charlotte Shillits, widow with four children, a lodger and a servant. 1884: Charles John Carr (directory) 1891: Household heads: Henry Christopher; Arthur Blake; Charles Brett (census) 1898: Richard Broadley (directory) 1901: Household heads: Emma Broadley; Kate Randall; Percival Maynard (census)
1926	Freehold sold by Rhodes estate to Henry Edward Austin, Albert Court, South Kensington
1931	Freehold sold to Abraham Goldstine, 230 Whitechapel Road, London

---

1   Tithe Map, photographic copy at London Metropolitan Archives.
2   Copies of the Renumbering Notices exist in Hackney Archives Department, LBH/7/8/1 and the London Metropolitan Archives, LCC/AR/BA/5/86. In this case, the single house, 1 Malvern Cottages became 3 Malvern Road, while nos. 2-3, 4-5 and 6-7 Malvern Cottages became 5, 7; 9, 11 and 13, 15 Malvern Road.
3   Hackney Archives Department, D/F/RHO/8; M4513.
4   London Metropolitan Archives, Middlesex Deeds Registry 1851 vol. 11/58-9.
5   Middlesex Deeds Registry 1852 vol. 7/862-3.
6   The London Metropolitan Archives hold a long series of London directories, mainly on microfilm. In principle, church rate books could be used for establishing the sequence of tenants, but for Hackney they only exist for the period 1853-60 and the way they are arranged makes them very difficult to use to follow the names of occupants.
7   Middlesex Deeds Registry 1853 vol. 5, 928-9

8   The dates of enrolment in the deed registry are not at all informative. One example noticed in the 1850 volume was for an 1841 lease.

9   Hackney Archives Department, D/F/RHO/5/3 and /RHO/6

10   The £20 per house referred to in the notebook might be such a cash payment. The rent of £5 per house would be equivalent to a lump sum payment of about £100.

11   Middlesex Deed Registry 1851 vol. 20/216; vol. 11/59; vol. 8/882

12   For 3 Caroline Cottages, Albert Road (Hackney Archives Department M4513), James Stanborough seems never to received the lease to which he was entitled by his agreement. Instead, the house was leased directly to the new purchaser by the Rhodes brothers with his consent. In contrast, Liscombe's leases were issued and he then sub-let the properties.

13   A search between 1862 and 1877 in the Deed Registry for the assignment of the lease either by Pritchard or Burt failed to find any relevant references.

14   These years were sampled in the electoral registers for Hackney Central Division at London Metropolitan Archives. Registers for 1911 and 1931 showed no qualified voters in the house.

15   In principle, it would be possible to identify this number by searching through the Valuation Books held by Hackney Archives Department (D/P1/4/1-3) for the entry for 9 Malvern Road.

16   If the 1926 deed had come to light at the beginning of the research rather than the end, it would, of course, have provided evidence for the original building date, though the search in the Middlesex Deed Registry would still have been needed to discover the details of Liscombe's lease. The 1931 sale also included a covenant, so again a copy could be obtained from the Registry, but no other transactions could be confirmed in this way. Some later information may become available after October 2003 (see p. 27).

4. Bricks Without Straw

Clifford Cottage (19 Clifford Chambers), Gloucestershire (now Warwickshire)

This case study shows how with perseverance and good fortune a full history of a house can be put together from scattered references, in the absence of the normal map, succession or deed evidence. With hindsight, some short cuts would have been possible and the discovery of one document at an earlier stage (noted below) would have given reassurance that the ownership being established was actually correct.

The house being researched stands in the village street of Clifford Chambers and is one half of a timber-framed house of three rooms in plan, later divided into two cottages and refronted in brick (Fig. 8.7); their modern names are Clifford and Avon Cottage (nos. 19 and 18 Clifford Chambers, respectively). The house incorporates fragmentary remains of fourteenth century timber-framing (probably the cross-wing of a substantial building), but is predominantly of the seventeenth century. The structure suggests a typical development for a village cottage: starting as a prosperous farmhouse but moving gradually down the social scale, as the village farms were consolidated into larger holdings. The enclosure of the open fields (1779 in Clifford Chambers) allowed new farms to be built away from the village and eventually the village farms were stripped of their farmland and became cottages. The history of such houses can be particularly difficult to establish, because of the problem of linking back to the period before they ceased to be farmhouses.

As a parish, Clifford Chambers is difficult to research. It has no early estate map, no enclosure map and a tithe map that only covers church property. Post-1832 Land Tax assessments have not survived in Gloucestershire, unlike Warwickshire, so sequences of owners are also difficult to establish.[1]

Fig. 8.7: Clifford Cottage (right) and the adjoining Avon Cottage (left), Nos. 19 and 18 Clifford
Chambers, Warwickshire (photo: N W Alcock).

The starting point

The first firm evidence identified for Clifford Cottage was the 1951 sale catalogue for the
Clifford Chambers Manor Estate, in which no. 19 was described as a brick and tiled
cottage.[2] Among many other properties in the village, the sale also covered the other half
of the house (no. 18) and Clifford Lodge, an adjoining substantial eighteenth-century
house. The layout shown in the map included with the sale catalogue strongly suggested
that nos. 18-19 had at some time been part of a larger property that included Clifford
Lodge (cf. Fig. 8.8). The title deeds started only in 1960 with the splitting of no. 19 from
no. 18, and any preceding deeds were not accessible. The 1951 sale catalogue gave a list
of 'roots of title', indicating that the estate had mostly been acquired between 1909 and
1919 (including the manor itself in 1911, bought from the West family of Alscot).
Unfortunately, searches in local record offices and inquiries of the solicitors produced no
trace of these purchase deeds. As a first approach, the possibility that the house had been
part of the Manor estate for a long period was considered. The West family archive at
WCRO (cf Case study 1) includes deeds for the manor itself, 1562-1793 (CR539/166),
and an important 1868 family settlement (CR2189/2), which listed their property in
Clifford Chambers in detail, including twelve cottages, although, frustratingly, their
occupiers were not named, and the map apparently associated with this deed could not
be found. Thus, at this point I could not establish if Clifford Cottage had belonged to the
manor.

Proceeding more cautiously, the 1910 'Domesday' evidence was examined. The
hereditament map identifies nos. 18-19, several other cottages and Clifford Lodge
together as hereditament 64, and the Field Book gave the owner as Mrs E A Smalman;
her property comprised a house, two cottages, buildings and land totalling 11 ac 8 p.[3]

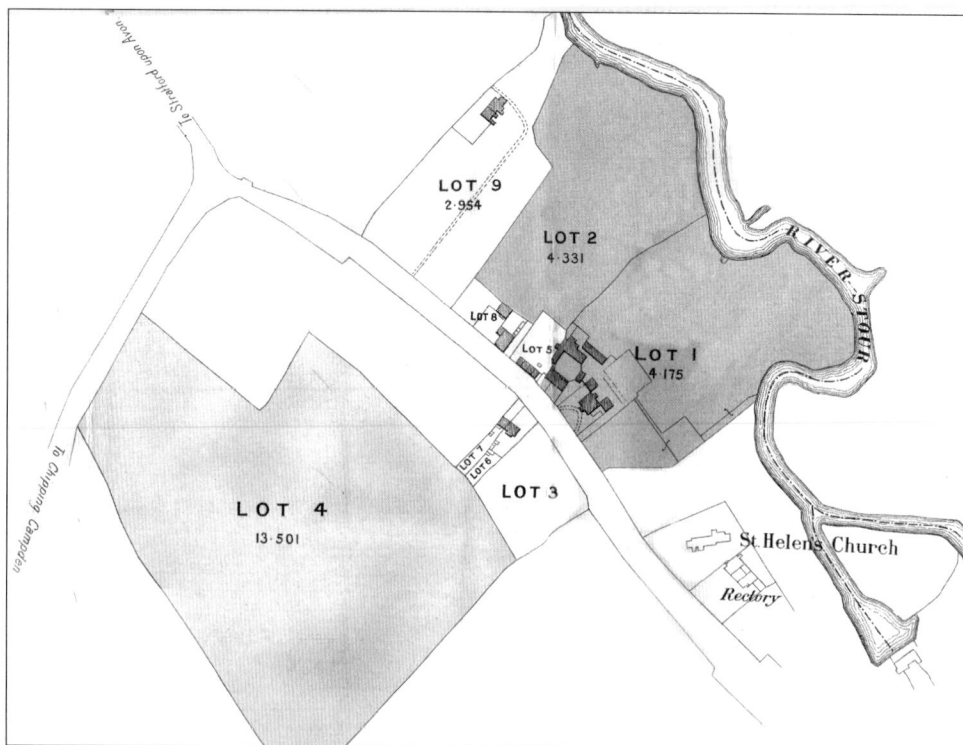

Fig. 8.8: 1906 sale catalogue map for property in Clifford Chambers (SBTRO DR165/841).
Nos 1-19 are the cottages set back from the road below the text 'Lot 5'. Clifford Lodge is Lot 1.

The purchase by the estate could now be identified with that from Herbert Spencer Smalman mentioned in the 1951 sale catalogue (17th Sept 1912). Clearly, therefore, the house had not previously belonged to the West family.

The sequence of owners

With the indication from the maps that it would be useful to search for Clifford Lodge as well as Clifford Cottage, progress became possible. An initial survey of sources showed that SBTRO held a considerable number of deed, estate and manorial records for Clifford, and one of the first items examined was a sale catalogue of 1880 that gave a real clue.[4] It related to property adjoining Clifford Lodge and its map marked the latter as belonging to 'Executors of late Mrs Hartshorn'. The ownership of Clifford Lodge by Mrs Susanna Hartshorne (the normal spelling) was confirmed from other evidence, and with this fixed point, various sources that listed owners and/or occupiers in the parish could be examined. The most useful is a series of annual poor rate assessments, which are very detailed for 1838-1861 (with less detail back to 1810). Land Tax assessments cover the period 1777-1832 and a further Poor Rate series extends from 1749 to 1779.[5]

The poor rate for 1861 lists 'Mrs Hartshorn', firstly for a house occupied by Richard Clarke (identifiable as Clifford Lodge), then for 5 acres of land and another house and 18½ acres and, later in the assessment, for six cottages, one of which was presumably Clifford Cottage. The evidence obtained by following the rate assessments back is summarised in Table 8.4.

Table 8.4 Land Tax and Poor Rate assessments for Clifford Lodge and adjoining property

Date	Owner	Occupier	Source*	Tax
1851-61	Mrs Hartshorne	herself and others	PR	
1839	– Nash esq.	Ralph Smith	PR	
1838-9	Nashes land	unstated	PR	
1821-1832	J. Nash	Ralph Smith	LT	£2
1800-1810	J. Nash	John Wyatt	LT	£2
1810-1815	Nashes land	John Wyatt		
(a) 1793-1798 (b) 1793-1821	John Parry Miss Wright	John Wyatt William Buller	LT	£2 £8
1778-1792	John Parry	John Wyatt	LT	£10
1777	John Parry	one entry for 'Smart's land', one presumably his own (£5 each),	LT	£10
1779	John Parry	house; his land; Smart land; Dighton's land	PR	
1769	John Parry	Richard Spiers (and other entries)	PR	
1749	(unstated)	Richard Spiers	PR	

* PR = Poor Rate. LT = Land Tax. For easy comparison, the Land Tax assessments have been converted to the standard 4s per £1 rate when the original rate was different.

In summary, the various tax and rate assessments allow an overview of the owners and major tenants for what can later be recognised as Clifford Lodge and Clifford Cottage. It is worth noting that they do not identify clearly who was living in the cottage in the 19th century. Fortunately, because the village comprises one long street, the households in the census enumerations were in street order and could be correlated from one decade to the next, taking the known tenants of Clifford Lodge as a starting point. Thus, it was possible to identify the cottage tenants with reasonable confidence.

The Parry, Nash and Hartshorne families

In seeking evidence about Susanna Hartshorne, the memorial inscriptions at Clifford Chambers were found to include a very informative tablet which confirmed the link between the Hartshorne, Nash and Parry families (see fig. 8.9). John Nash (1760-1839) had two wives of whom the first, Elizabeth Harris, was descended from the Parry family. His second, Susanna Bourne, married Thomas Hartshorne after John's death. Thus, the series of owners revealed by the rate and tax assessments were all members of the same family. Although little has been discovered about Thomas Hartshorne, Susanna's death was of sufficient note to be mentioned in the Times as 'A centenarian', noting that she survived her second husband for many years and that up to a few weeks before her death, she was to be seen walking with an attendant in the streets of Worcester.[6] With the date of death established, it was possible to locate her will. It listed extensive property in Worcester and her estate at Clifford Chambers all of which was left to her relative, William Nash Skillicorne. The will of John Nash of St Martin, Worcester dated 13th Sept 1826 left all his estates to his wife Susanna.[7] The parish registers for Clifford Chambers included the marriage of Joseph Harris with Sarah Parry in 1758 (the parents of Elizabeth Harris who married John Nash) but had no other relevant entries.

A check of the extensive personal name index at SBTRO revealed two significant Parry references. The first was a deed that proved to refer to Clifford Cottage itself. On 2 Sept 1794, John Parry of Clifford Chambers, gentleman, released to John Nash of Worcester, surgeon and Elizabeth his wife (formerly Elizabeth Harris, spinster, niece of John Parry), a *messuage* [house], stable and buildings occupied by John Parry, and a *farmhouse*, yards, stables and wagon houses with two pieces of arable land, and one piece of pasture land (total 19 acres), all occupied by John Wyatt.[8] From this, the relationship became clear between the later Clifford Lodge, the gentleman's house (John Parry), and the farmhouse (John Wyatt). From the census and Poor Rate evidence, the farmhouse was probably divided into two cottages occupied by agricultural labourers in the 1830s.

The second document was the will of Joseph Parry (I) of Clifford Chambers, dated 1758.[9] He left an 'estate in Clifford Chambers devised by my brother John Parry, deceased' to his son Joseph (II). His eldest son was John (III) and he also had daughters Rebecca and Sarah, the wife of Joseph Harris. The next task, to locate the will of Joseph's brother John Parry, proved very frustrating. Wills proved at Gloucester included those of Joseph Parry (I) himself and of Rebecca (see next section), but the only John (1749) proved to be the wrong person. Worcester diocese wills included no likely John, while wills proved in the Prerogative Court (PRO) included twelve John Parrys back to 1727, one from Warwickshire (again incorrect) but none from Gloucestershire. Working backwards systematically through these had progressed to 1743 without success when, finally, a check of the very sparse name index in WCRO located the 1737 will of John Parry, of St James, Westminster, among deeds for a farm in Charlecote, Warwickshire.[10]

He proved to be the brother of Joseph (I) and his will supplied extensive information about his family, as well as mentioning the Clifford Chambers property. His first request was for his body to be buried in the chancel of 'Somertiles Aston', Gloucestershire (*sic*, for Aston Somerville), and he made bequests to his wife Mary, brother Joseph and Elizabeth the widow of his brother Henry, as well as numerous other relatives, nephews, nieces, cousins etc.

Specifically, he left 'my messuage now let to Richard Spiers in Clifford Chambers', with an orchard, a close and two yardlands of arable land, to his wife Mary for her life, and then to Joseph (I). Most frustratingly, although he identified the former owners of all the other property he bequeathed, he made no mention of it for the Clifford Chambers property. This omission suggested that it might be inherited family property.

The mention of Aston Somerville in John Parry (II)'s will led to a description of the family monuments in the chancel there.[11] These indicated that his parents were John Parry (I), rector of that parish (1639-1714) and Rebecca Fulwood, daughter of 'Thomas Fulwood of Warwickshire'. The IGI identified their marriage on 9th Sept 1664 at Aston Cantlow, Warwickshire, and her baptism there on 7th October 1638. From this, her father was recognised as Thomas Fulwood, a land-owner in Little Alne, a hamlet in the parish of Aston Cantlow, whose family is included in the 1680 Visitation of Warwickshire.[12] Had he owned the Clifford Chambers property?

Various strands of evidence that might have identified John Parry (II)'s predecessors were examined without success. Glebe terriers for 1635 and 1677 give detailed lists of the strips in the open fields belonging to the church including the names of every owner/tenant of adjoining land.[13] They list seven and eleven villagers respectively, but include neither Parry nor Fulwood, and the only later terrier post-dates the enclosure so lacks names that might have been correlated with these early ones. Seventeenth century deeds survive for several properties belonging to these villagers, some of which are part of sequences continuing to after 1737 (and so not acquired by John Parry); but they do not give enough evidence to identify his predecessor by elimination. An 1806 glebe terrier has a list of those responsible for repairing the churchyard wall, showing that John Nash was responsible for 10 ft.[14] Unfortunately, the earlier terriers do not give similar lists which could be correlated with the later evidence. A dead end had been reached, with apparently just a few loose ends left to be tied up.

Rebecca Parry and the Clifford Chambers Enclosure Award

A comparison between John Parry's will and the 1794 deed showed that by the latter date, the Parry property had been greatly diminished in size, from two yardlands in 1737 (about 60 acres) to 20 acres. Would the history of the remainder of John's property be of any help? In the 1779 Enclosure Award for Clifford Chambers,[15] allotments were made to seven owners, surprisingly including Rebecca rather than Joseph Parry (II); she received two allotments in lieu of a four-yardland holding. The 1787 will of Rebecca Parry, spinster of Clifford Chambers, records the bequest of her messuages and land at Clifford Chambers to her brother John, who was her executor.[16] Thus, it seemed likely that she was indeed the owner of John Parry's farm. This was confirmed from the first of her two allotments at enclosure. From the description, it was recognisable as the arable land transferred by John Parry to John Nash in 1794.

From the award, her larger allotment (133 acres) lay on the western side of the parish, to the south of allotments to Samuel Morris and William Taplin. A group of title deeds covering the latter two properties, including a plan of 1867, shows that they became Clifford Hill Farm.[17] Rebecca Parry's allotment therefore became the later Leys Farm, (or Starveall Farm) adjoining this to the south. The 1910 Valuation Book showed the owner of Leys Farm to be Thomas Hopkins Hodges of Long Marston,[18] and it seemed worthwhile to search for deeds for it, that might contain Parry information. However, the present owner had no early deeds.

The Slatter, Son and More deeds

The name T H Hodges of Long Marston was slightly familiar from a different project in which some information about him had come to light in a solicitors collection that had not shown up in the indexes under Clifford Chambers. The brief list of the collection did indeed mention T H Hodges, but the first discovery in this list was about 20 further document bundles for Clifford Chambers. Most of these related to probate of wills but a few concerned property and it seemed they might perhaps be useful for understanding the pattern of ownership in the village (through mentions of the owners of adjacent land, etc). Remarkably, however, one of the bundles contained the draft deeds and abstract compiled for the sale of Clifford Lodge and associated property (including the two cottages) from William Nash Skillicorne to R S Smith in 1890.[19] These fully confirmed the sequence of ownership that had been established from the sources described above, starting with the 1794 deed between John Parry (III) and John Nash. They also showed in detail how Nash had built up a block of property in the middle of the village (involving five separate purchases). Of course, if this bundle of papers had come to light at the beginning of the research, it would have documented the whole nineteenth century house history at a stroke.

A further search for Clifford Chambers at SBTRO then found documentation for the next stage in the ownership of Clifford Lodge and its cottages, its 1906 sale following the death of R S Smith as well as a copy of the particulars for this sale with a map (Fig. 8.8).[20] The property was auctioned in several lots, of which Clifford and Avon Cottages made up lot 2.

The deed bundle in the same solicitor's collection indexed under the name of 'T H Hodges of Long Marston' proved to concern his sale of Leys Farm in Clifford Chambers, despite the absence of any mention of this village in the list entry.[21] It includes in particular an abstract of title starting with the sale on 28-29 September 1792 by John Parry to Elizabeth Wright of nine fields making up the main enclosure allotment to Rebecca Parry (the later Leys Farm). Because this property was of considerably larger value than his remaining property, Elizabeth Wright was to have the title deeds and covenanted to keep them safe, *and the abstract includes a list of these deeds*. Although the list only gives the dates and parties, it was possible to work out with considerable confidence what transactions were involved. The first group of deeds in the list related to a two-yardland farm, 'Smart's Land' which was bought by Rebecca Parry in 1773 (as seen in the 1777 Land Tax Assessment). They were followed by deeds relating to the two yardlands belonging to John Parry (II). This sequence started with two deeds of 1650-51 by which the farm was bought by one Thomas Hobbins from Henry Rainsford, lord of the manor of Clifford Chambers. It descended in the Hobbins family until 1699, when it apparently passed to Christopher Owen, and then in 1713 was acquired by Henry Parry and his wife Elizabeth (who was perhaps either a Hobbins or an Owen). In 1720 it was bought by Henry's brother, John Parry (II), and descended as already discovered to John Parry (III). Thus, even though the original documents did not survive, this list of deeds provides the link which I had failed to find in other sources, to carry the story of Clifford Cottage back to John Parry (II)'s predecessors.

The earliest transaction in the list has a clear context. In the late 1640s, Henry Rainsford, the lord of the manor, was in deep financial trouble because a heavy fine was imposed on him as a Royalist. He sold the manor of Clifford Chambers to Job Dighton in 1649 and at the same time was selling off individual parts of the estate, including Heath Fields (which became Hines House) (Case Study 1). In 1650, as part of the sale of the manor, Henry Rainsford assigned a mortgage to trustees for Dighton; however, the village farms covered by the mortgage had already been sold to other people, so the trustees had to hold this part of the estate in trust for the new owners. As a result, the deed gives a complete overview of property in the village.[22] It describes nine farms, two of 2 yardlands (one bought for Thomas Hobbins), one of 1$\frac{1}{2}$ yardlands, three of 1 yardland and three of $\frac{1}{2}$ yardland; the deeds for the manor itself included eleven cottages which had not been sold. Thus, Thomas Hobbins's farm was one of the two largest in the village.

A 1623 lease also exists, of a messuage and 2 yardlands, made by Henry Rainsford to John Hobbins, his son Henry and wife Margaret, for their lives.[23] This shows that the Hobbins family had previously been tenants of the farm they bought in 1650. The lease includes an unusual condition, that Henry (then 33) was

> 'to attend and bee ready with a nagge, horse or mare to ride with him the said Henry Raynsford when hee shall bee thereunto requested, the said Henry Hobbins having his livery cloake or coate allowed unto him by the said Henry Raynsford'.

The Hobbins family

With the Hobbins family identified as the seventeenth century tenants and then owners, their family history could be investigated through the Clifford registers, wills and other documents. These produced considerable evidence about the family and only a few of the highlights are mentioned here. The evidence for the family starts with what is known either as the 1522 'military survey', or 'muster'.[24] This lists everyone over the age of 16 with their wealth, either in land or in goods. Officially, its purpose was to identify how much people should contribute to the furnishing of arms for war with France. However, it was in reality a subterfuge of Cardinal Wolsey to obtain realistic values of peoples' wealth, as a preliminary to forced loans and subsidy payments (which were implemented in 1522 and 1523).[25] For Clifford Chambers, the list includes Thomas Hobbyns, one of the most wealthy of the seven tenants listed. Wills from 1562, 1627, 1648 and 1685 carry the story forward to the end of the seventeenth century.[26] That of Henry Hobbins in 1648 (the one who had to ride with Henry Raynsford) is significant for the house history, as he made an unusual provision.

> After my decease, the chamber next the streete in the new buildinge of the said messuage shalbe equally divided into to [two] partes at the coste & charges of my executor [his son] and my executor permit my loving wife Elleanor Hobins to elect and choose which halfe of the said chamber she shall like best and from thenceforth during her widowhood hould and enjoy the same together with one of the bedsteds in the said chamber which she shall choose, with the feather bedd and boulsters there with sheetes, blankettes and all other furniture necessary for the same … and my will is that my wife shall have … provided by my executor during her widowhood convenient fuell for her use and the free use and liberty of the fier and fierplaces and of such goodes and vessells which I leave to my executor which shall be useful for her about the fier.

Thus in the absence of a probate inventory, this will provides the best documentary evidence for Clifford Cottage in the seventeenth century; the 'new building' probably refers to the rebuilding of one bay of the cottage which can be dated to about this period. The 1671-2 Hearth Tax assessment includes Thomas Hobbins with two hearths in his house, presumably the back-to-back fireplaces in the main chimney of the house.[27]

Unusually for someone of yeoman status, Thomas Hobbins appears in three late seventeenth century Chancery law suits; these could be identified through the PRO on-line catalogue because Hobbins is a sufficiently unusual name.[28] The first involved him as one of the 'Town Proctors' of Clifford Chambers, the people appointed to administer the village's assets; he held the post from 1658 to 1666, jointly with William Cale. Unfortunately, he failed to agree his accounts with Cale and the latter sued him to recover the unpaid balance for which they were liable. The second case relates to the business dealings of one John Woodin who had brought a large amount of coal up the river Avon to a wharf in Stratford. It appears that the plaintiff in the case, one William Hunt, had invested £300 as Woodin's partner in the trade, while Thomas Hobbins had lent Woodin £50 and in due course had this repaid. However, Hunt considered that he should have been paid rather than Hobbins, and was suing the latter for this money. The last case was more personal, involving a claim for the fraudulent sale of the property of the father of Sarah Hobbins, Thomas's wife.

Before the sixteenth century

Very few documents relating to Clifford Chambers have survived from before the early sixteenth century, and none show the tenants of the village farms. The previous history of the house therefore has to be inferred. As we have seen, in the later sixteenth century it was the house for a two yardland farm held from the manor of Clifford. A survey of the manor taken in 1266-7, shows a typical social structure for the period.[29] The village included one farm of four virgates (yardlands), held by Robert le Freman (thus probably a freeholding), four one virgate freeholdings, and seventeen villein holdings of one virgate, as well as a number of cottages. That the Hobbins farm was leased from the manor in 1623 (above) indicates that it was a villein holding rather than a freeholding. This lease also required the payment on the death of a tenant of not one but two 'heriots' (payments on a tenant's death, usually the 'best beast' or its value in money), strongly suggesting that the farm had been formed by the combination of two one yardland holdings. Thus when Clifford Cottage was built in the fourteenth century it probably belonged to one of the one-virgate villein holdings and was combined with a second yardland during the period of declining prosperity after the Black Death.

The family ownership of Clifford Cottage is summarised in Table 8.5.

Table 8.5 Ownership summary for Clifford Cottage, Clifford Chambers

Date	Family ownership
Pre-1522	One-yardland villein holding, later enlarged to two yardlands
Pre-1522-1699	Hobbins family
1713-1794	Parry family
1794-1890	Nash, Hartshorne and Skillicorne families.
c. 1830	Farmhouse divided into two cottages
1890-1906	R S Smith
1906-1912	Smalman family
1912-1951	Cottage belonging to Clifford Chambers Manor estate

Table 8.6 Parry, Nash and Hartshorne family tree

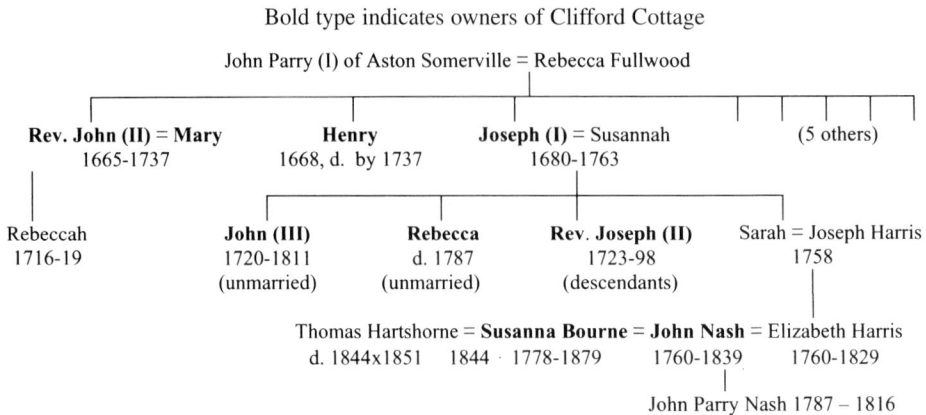

Bold type indicates owners of Clifford Cottage

John Parry (I) of Aston Somerville = Rebecca Fullwood

Rev. John (II) = Mary	**Henry**	**Joseph (I) = Susannah**	(5 others)
1665-1737	1668, d. by 1737	1680-1763	

Rebeccah	**John (III)**	**Rebecca**	**Rev. Joseph (II)**	Sarah = Joseph Harris
1716-19	1720-1811	d. 1787	1723-98	1758
	(unmarried)	(unmarried)	(descendants)	

Thomas Hartshorne = **Susanna Bourne** = **John Nash** = Elizabeth Harris
d. 1844x1851   1844 · 1778-1879   1760-1839   1760-1829

John Parry Nash 1787 – 1816

1   As for Hines House (Case Study 1), some relevant records had to be looked for in Gloucestershire RO but most were in WCRO or SBTRO.

2   WCRO EAC111.

3   Map: PRO IR129/8/218(1). Field Book: PRO IR58/89329-30. The description is confusing as hereditaments 17, 18, 65, 66, 69 and 121 were also included under the same valuation but only 64 and 69 were shown on the map. Such combinations are often found in the Field Books, but can sometimes be clarified from the Valuation Books which do list all the hereditaments individually.

4   SBTRO DR153/43

5   Poor Rates: WCRO DR325/65-78; Land Tax: Gloucester RO.

6   Times, July 2nd 1879, p. 4 col. f

7   Susanna Hartshorne, Birmingham Probate Registry, 1879; John Nash, PRO PROB 11/1919, s.703, f.17

8   SBTRO DR648/50, a copy deed. This is John Parry (III) in the family tree (Table 8.6).

9   SBTRO DR648/2. Joseph (I) died in 1763.

10 WCRO L6/126.

11 Printed in Ralph Bigland, *Historical, monumental and genealogical collections relative to the county of Gloucester* (ed. Brian Frith from the original eighteenth century manuscripts), Gloucestershire Record Series ; vol. 2. Alan Sutton, 1989.

12 Harleian Society, 1911, *Visitation of the County of Warwick ...1682*, Ed. W. H. Rylands.

13 Gloucestershire RO 82T 1/64/1-2.

14 WCRO DR325/23. This is a 'panel list', as described above (p. 19).

15 WCRO DR325/122. The award was implemented in 1781.

16 Gloucestershire RO 1787/77. It is not clear why John rather than Rebecca Parry is listed in the Land Tax assessments and Poor Rates before her death. It may be that he was running the farm for her and he probably lived with her at Clifford Lodge.

17 SBTRO DR149/175

18 WCRO CR1978/1/29.

19 WCRO CR1596/868.

20 SBTRO DR153/587-8 and DR164/841.

21 WCRO CR1596/532.

22 The sale to Dighton is in the West estate documents (WCRO CR539/66), but this assignment is in a separate group of Clifford documents, SBTRO DR140/8.

23 SBTRO DR33/10.

24 At Berkeley Castle (Book 27) and on microfilm at the Bodleian Library.

25 See Julian Cornwall, *Wealth and Society in Early Sixteenth Century England*, Routledge and Kegan Paul, 1988, for a full discussion of the 1522 muster. For those counties where it survives, it is a very valuable source both for individuals and for village social structure.

26 Gloucestershire RO 1562/64 and 1627/108; PRO PROB11/210, s.174 (dated 1648, proved 1649) and PROB 11/379, s. 45 (1685).

27 Gloucestershire RO D383

28 PRO C5/458/25; C5/503/24; C5/86/14 and C5/500/4.

29 W H Hart, *Historia et cartularium monasterii Sancti Petri Gloucestriae*, vol. iii, Rolls Series, 1867, p. 49.

5. Life in the House

1-2 Stareton, Warwickshire

Stareton is a hamlet of half-a-dozen houses in the parish of Stoneleigh in which this pair of brick-fronted estate cottages stand (Fig. 8.9). From the front, they appear to be of the late eighteenth century, but the end gables and the rear wall show fragmentary timber-framing indicating an earlier origin. Internally, it can be seen that most of the original structure survives of a house of two rooms in plan, having a 'lobby entry' (Fig. 8.10); this plan type has its central door leading directly to a lobby between the two rooms and the narrow staircase is set opposite the front door, at the side of the chimney. It has two full

Fig. 8.9: Nos. 1-2 Stareton, Warwickshire (photo: N. W. Alcock).

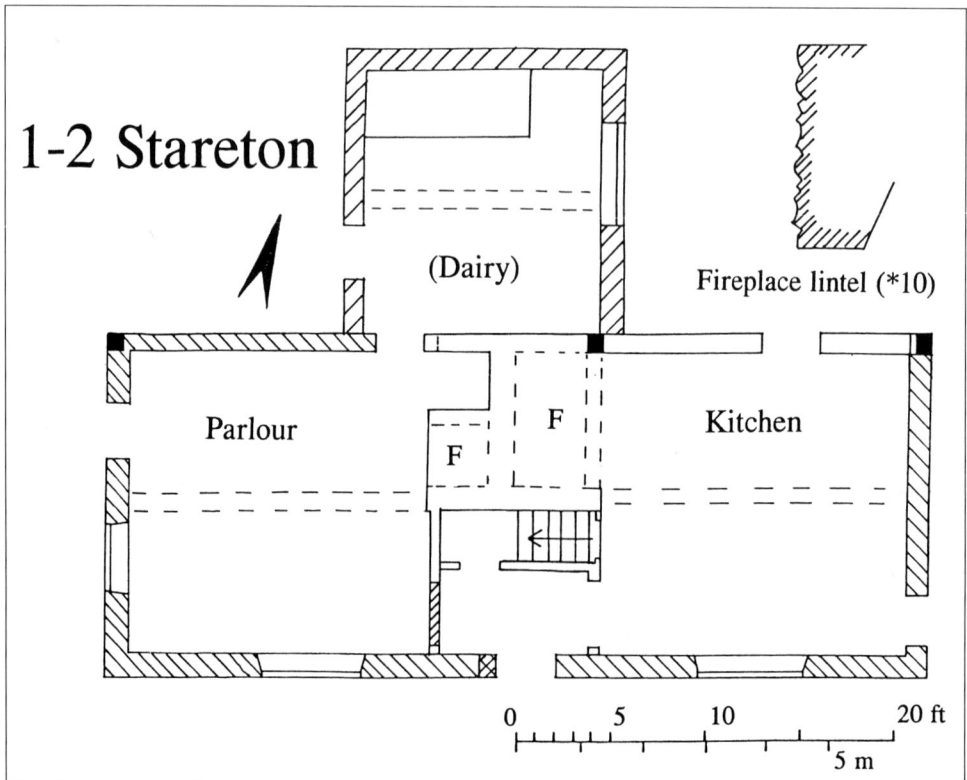

Fig. 8.10: Plan of 1-2 Stareton, from N W Alcock, *People at Home*, Phillimore, 1993.

storeys with attics above. A brick rear wing gives the house an overall T-plan; the evidence of an original first floor doorway indicates that this wing replaces an earlier one. A construction date of the later seventeenth century is indicated by the details of the timber-framing, by the presence of attics (a relatively late feature) and by the 'lobby entry' plan, a form only introduced in Warwickshire after the Civil War.[1]

The house belongs to the Stoneleigh Abbey estate for which exceptionally good records survives.[2] It was quickly established that the house served a small farm of around 30 acres (12 ha) until the nineteenth century, when it was divided into two cottages, as it still remains. Because its history formed part of a wider documentary study of the parish, it was not restricted to the period after the house was built but was carried back as far as possible.[3] The sixteenth and early seventeenth century evidence proved to be exceptionally informative about developments in housing standards in the region.

As a first step in establishing the history of the house, it can be identified on maps of 1854, 1766, 1683 and 1597. The 1597 map identifies the house as a freeholding belonging to the Coventry Guild of Blacksmiths but in the following year it was bought by Sir Thomas Leigh.[4] Earlier estate rentals show that the blacksmiths had to pay a quit-rent of 1lb of cumin and the cartulary of Stoneleigh Abbey (the *Stoneleigh Leger Book*) includes a copy of the thirteenth century grant of the freehold by the lord of the manor of Stareton to one Peter Aleyn, paying this rent.[5] A search in the Coventry City Archives located two deeds relating to the farm. The first contains its gift to the guild in 1529 to support prayers for the dead.[6] The second was a thirty-one year lease made in 1555 by the Coventry Blacksmiths Guild to Thomas Tuter of Stareton, husbandman. This included an interesting condition, significant for the chronology of sixteenth century house modernisation. Within two years, he had to:

> build and set up in the said messuage one chymney of stone, and make a chamber flower over one parler ther of tymber and bordes with dors and wyndowes to the same.[7]

Other sixteenth century tenants were identified from incidental references in the Stoneleigh manorial documents to residents in Stareton who were not tenants of the Abbey estate. after its purchase by Sir Thomas Leigh, estate rentals provide a sequence of tenant's names up to 1645 and from 1697 to the twentieth century. The gap in the later seventeenth century can be filled partly by the 1680 map and partly from a series of 'suitor lists' (Fig. 8.11); these annual lists of tenants owing suit to (required to attend) the manor court were often updated by crossing out the names of tenants who had left or died and substituting the new name. From the sequence of tenants, a remarkable series of wills and probate inventories relating to the house can be identified and, as an aid to understanding the development of the house, most of the inventories list its rooms (Table 8.7).

Thus, the history of the *farm* has been established for an exceptionally long period. For the house itself, we have the evidence both of its structure and of the descriptions in the inventories, to indicate that it must have been rebuilt after 1560 – perhaps more than once. The enlargement that took place in about 1600 was typical for the period.[8] It involved the addition of upper rooms and extra service rooms (a dairy [the *mylke house*] and a *boulting house*, for sieving flour), to a house of medieval form with just three ground floor rooms. The late seventeenth century rebuilding was also characteristic of its period. It used a much more compact plan, with all the bed-chambers upstairs (see below) and included an attic storey.

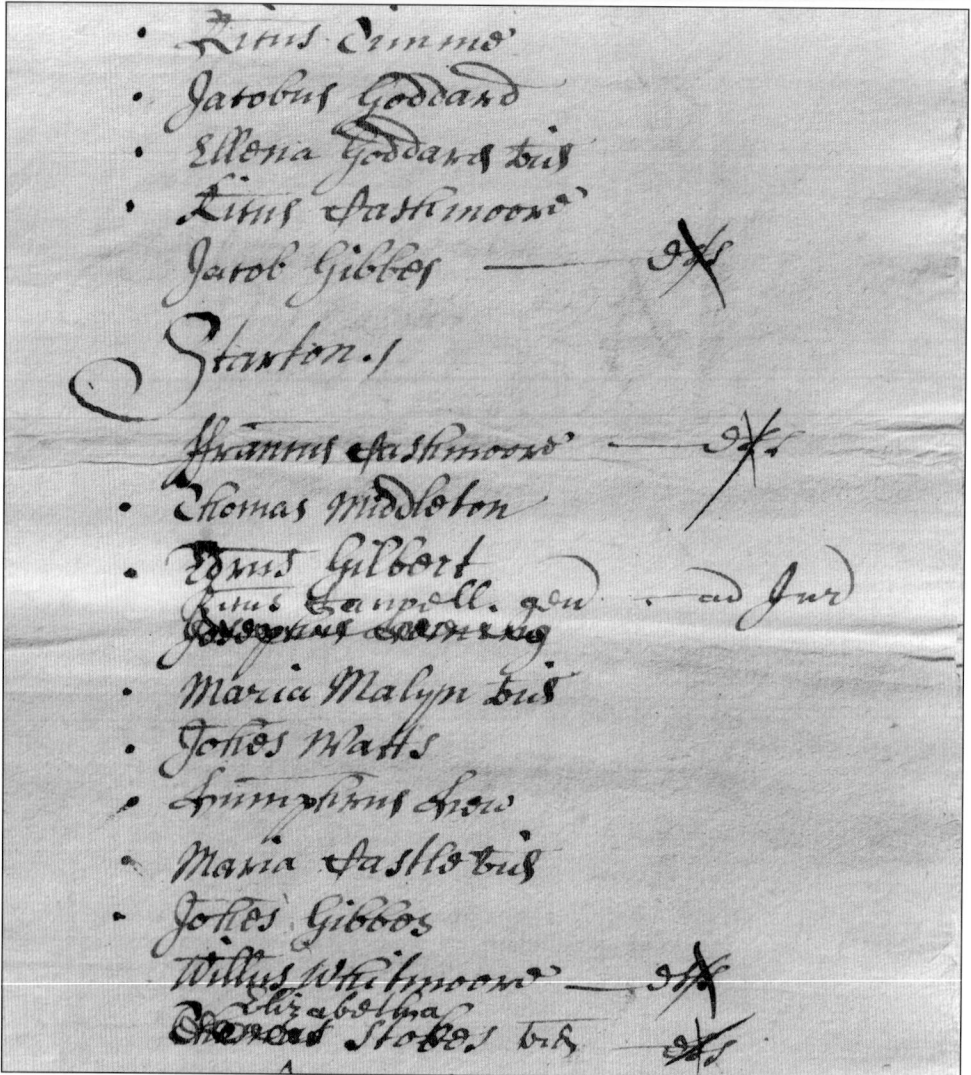

Fig. 8.11 List of tenants owing suit to (required to attend) the Stoneleigh manor court on 30th September 1686 (extract). In the Stareton list, the substitution of Richard Canpell (Camill), gentleman, for Joseph Heming can be seen near the top (SBTRO DR18/30/24/463).

The key to understanding this modernisation and the choice of the up-to-date plan comes from another deed in the estate archives. In 1674, a life lease was granted to Richard Camill, servant to Lord Leigh, 'in consideration of his true service' and, as both the suitor list (Fig. 8.11) and his inventory show, he was considered to have the status of a 'gentleman'. When he gained possession of the house, after the death of Joseph Hemming in 1686, he must have rebuilt the house in its present form. Richard Camill married Elizabeth Holloway in 1683, and their eldest daughter, Sarah, was probably born soon afterwards. The baptisms of two other children are recorded, Holloway (1691) and Mary (July 1694). Richard died in 1693/4 and his widow succeeded him as tenant until her death in 1709, when Holloway followed her (at the tender age of 18). He held the farm until 1758, followed by his widow and grandson Thomas, tenant from 1775 until his death in 1815, a notable but not untypically long tenure for one family.

Table 8.7 Probate records for 1-2 Stareton, Stoneleigh.

Year	Name	Documents*	Rooms in inventory
1558	Thomas Tuter	WI	Hall, chamber (kitchen?)
1563	Ales Tuter	WI	(none listed)
1575	Simon Tyler	I	Parlor, Hall, Kechen
1616	Leonard Hemmings	WI	Hall, Bedchamber, Chambers above, Nether House, Boulting House, Mylke House; Barne
1640	John Heminges	WI	Chamber, Upper Chamber, Other Chamber, Hall House, Buttery, Nether Roome; Barne
1694	Richard Camill	I	His Bedchamber, Chamber over Kitchin, Another Chamber, Another Chamber, Cockloft, Parlour, Kitchin, Dayryhouse; Barne (PRO PROB4/25461)
1709	Elizabeth Cammill	WI	(none listed)
1758	Holloway Campbell	W	
1774	Mary Campbell	W	(dated 11th May 1768)
1816	Thomas Campbell	W	(dated 27th June 1815)

* W = Will; I = Probate inventory. Unless otherwise noted, the documents are at the Lichfield Joint Record Office, filed by date and name.

Richard's probate inventory of January 1694 fits very well with the layout of the house, giving a particularly clear sequence for the rooms. It is worth quoting this in full, (page 96), to illustrate the interpretation of such documents.[9]

To help understand the working of the house and the life of the Camill family, it has been possible to draw out the house with its contents (Fig. 8.12).[10] The appraisers started in Richard Camill's bedchamber. This was heated, and can be confidently identified with the first floor west room which has the only original upstairs fireplace. Its comfortable furnishings included two looking glasses, but nothing for storage. They then crossed the landing to the chamber over the kitchen, where his two children slept, Sarah (aged ten) and Holloway (three); the cradle here was ready for the next arrival (Mary, born six months later, in July 1694). Sarah was perhaps learning to read from the family bible and the other books the appraisers found here. This room must also have held most of the family's miscellaneous belongings, kept in a chest of drawers, two trunks and two boxes, though the linens were in a trunk in the chamber over the rear block (visited next). Up in the attics, one room was used as a corn and cheese chamber and held a substantial amount of wheat and rye (£8 worth); the inventory does not differentiate the 'wheat, rye and a parcell of chese', but in January this was likely to have been mainly corn, as cheese was usually sold in the autumn.[11] The other attic (the cockloft) held a bed, probably for a farm servant or apprentice; although no such member of the household is recorded, it seems very likely that Richard Camill needed regular help with the farm.

Downstairs, the two main rooms were no longer the previously standard combination: a living hall and a sleeping parlour. They had been transformed so that the parlour was the principal living room, furnished with two tables and six leather and four other chairs. It was a room where the family could gather comfortably and receive visitors, and this was one of the first small houses in the parish where the parlour had this

Richard's probate inventory of January 1694

Inventory of Richard Camill, gentleman, appraised by Edward Croft, Francis Casmore and Francis Clayton, 17 January 1693[/4]

	£	s	d
His wearing apparrell and money in his purse	10	0	0
In his Bedchamber			
One bedstead, a feather bed and boulster, two pillowes, a paire of blankets and a coverlid, six cheires, two stools, one blanket, two glasses, one paire of andirons, a fire shovell and tongues, and a paire of bellowes	6	18	0
In the Chamber over the Kitchen			
Two bedsteads, two featherbeds and boulsters, a rug and two paire of blankets with a sett of curtaines and vallance, a chest of drawers, two trunks, two boxes, a table, two chaires, two lookeing glases, a cradle, a great bible and severall other bookes	9	6	0
In another Chamber			
One trunck, one paire of Holland sheets, foure paire of flaxen sheets, foure paire of hempen sheets, three table cloaths, two dozen of hempen napkins, foure paire of pillow drawers, a diaper table cloath and one dozen of diaper napkins	7	0	0
In another Chamber			
Wheat and rye, a parcell of chese, one paire of bucketts and some other implements	8	15	0
Twelve pound of yarne		16	0
In the Cockloft			
One paire of bucskins, two paire of doe skins, a bedstead, a flockbed, a boulster, three blankets, two spinning wheels, a parcell of woollen yarne, a still and severall other implements	3	18	0
In the Parlour			
Two tables, six leather chaires, foure other chaires, a paire of andirons, fire shovell & tongues	2	0	0
In the Kitchin			
Three brasse kettles, two brasse potts, three skellets, a warming pan and a fryeing pan	2	10	0
Seaven pewter dishes, a cheese plate, a pye plate, two dozen of trenchers and plates, three fowling peeces and a jack	2	10	0
Two spitts, a dripping pan, a paire of racks, a paire of andirons, fire shovell & tongues, pot hookes and hangers		15	0
Foure chaires, a bacon rack, two tressel boards, a chopping knife, a cleaver and two tables		10	0
In the Dayryhouse			
A cheese presse, six barrells, two tubs, a churne, two kimnells, three pales, a dough cover [kiver], a trencher rack & 3 dozen of trenchers	1	10	0
2 Flitchins of bacon	1	0	0
Six milch cowes, 5 heifers, 2 calves	42	0	0
One mare or nag & a filly	13	6	8
Thirteene sheepe	6	10	0
Eleaven lambs	3	6	0
One hogg	2	0	0
A parcell of oats in the barne	2	10	0
A rick of hay and hay in the barne	7	0	0
Three acres of corne growing on the land	4	10	0
Nine silver spoones	3	0	0
Implements & other things forgotten		5	0
Debts sperate & desperate	201	0	0
Total	343	15	8

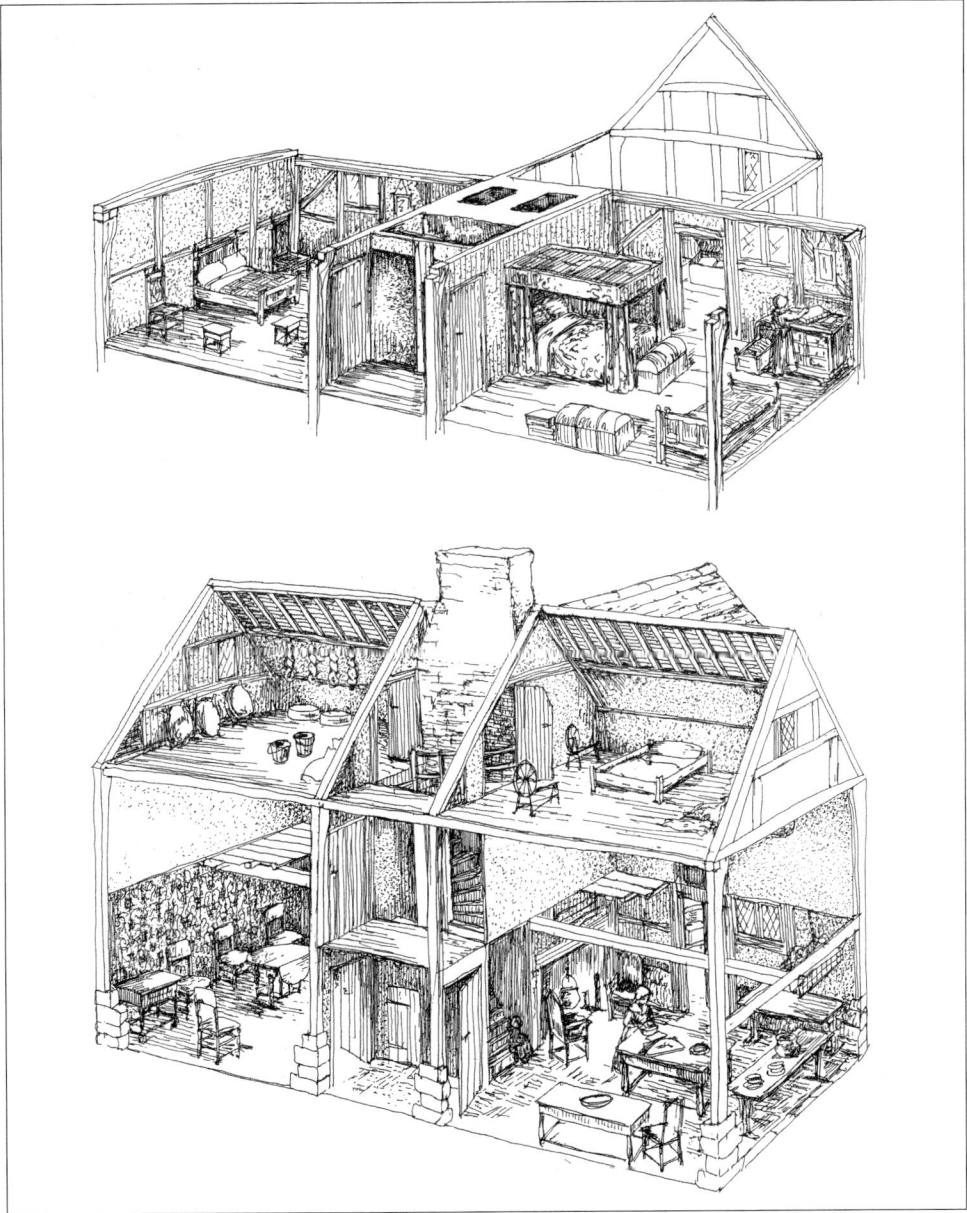

Fig. 8.12: Inventory reconstruction for 1-2 Stareton (a) Ground floor and attic (b) First floor (drawing by Dr Pat Hughes, from M. Locock (ed.), *Meaningful Architecture: Social Interpretation of Buildings*, Avebury, 1994).

role. At the same time as this change was taking place, the term 'hall' was going out of use, and the two principal rooms were generally called 'parlour' and kitchen' (as here). Richard Camill's kitchen was the centre for cooking and food preparation, with the dishes, plates, pots and pans, two dozen trenchers [wooden plates], fireplace fittings including pothooks and spits, trestle tables, a chopping knife and cleaver. The final room encountered was the dairy in the back wing, which held the dough kiver [wooden storage box for bread dough] as well as the churn and cheese press, and also a trencher rack and another three dozen trenchers. The Camill family were surprisingly backward in this respect. When they and their visitors dined (probably in the parlour), they must have eaten off wood rather than pewter, of which they had only seven dishes.

Despite the extensive estate documentation, the later stages in the house's development are somewhat obscure. The brick re-fronting can be dated stylistically to the later eighteenth century, possibly being done when Thomas Campbell took over the tenancy of the farm in 1775. A survey of 1813 (a couple of years before his death) still shows him as tenant, but an undated amendment to the survey notes 'Manly the carpenter occupies this homestead'. What seems to have happened is that some of the farms in Stareton hamlet had been reorganised; some of the land was added to other farms and the rest incorporated into the park.[12] The house became a farm cottage, probably that listed under Manly's name in the rentals from 1823 onwards, and in the 1841 census William Manly, carpenter, is the first person named in Stareton, followed by George and Elizabeth Jones; this sequence helps confirm the identification, as the house is the first one in the village when approaching it from the west. When the estate was again mapped and surveyed in 1854, the house had been combined with the adjacent farm, which was in the tenure of George Jones. Presumably it was being used as labourers' cottages.[13] As in the previous Case Study, careful correlation of the census returns with the estate documentation can help identify occupiers.

---

[1]   The most distinctive structural features are the pair of roof trusses on each side of the chimney; the principals of the western one have curved feet inset on the tiebeam (characteristic of late 17th century Warwickshire). The attic stairhead landing has an original simple curved railing with three square-sectioned rails halved across the stair newel posts. The kitchen fireplace lintel has a remarkable multiple moulding (Fig. 8.10, inset), probably of the 16th century, and this decoration presumably led to it being saved when the previous house was rebuilt. The present rear wing is probably the same date as the rebuilding of the front wall in brick. Its predecessor seems to have been entered from the kitchen and was therefore probably placed rather further east; consistent with this, there is a doorway at first floor level in the only visible surviving section of wall framing, in the rear wall of the eastern bay

[2]   Mainly in SBTRO DR18.

[3]   See N W Alcock, *People at Home*, Phillimore, 1993, esp. pp. 35-39.

[4]   SBTRO DR18/10/100.

[5]   R H Hilton (ed.), *The Stoneleigh Leger Book*, Dugdale Society, 1960, p.238. The identification of the blacksmith's freeholding with that granted to Peter Aleyn is confirmed by its being the only freeholding in Stareton.

[6]   Coventry RO BA/D/K/22/4. After the dissolution of the 'Guilds and Chantries', Coventry Corporation purchased all the former property of the city's guilds. Technically, the Stareton farm belonged to the Corporation, but they seem to have assigned it informally to the blacksmiths.

[7]   Coventry RO BA/D/A/56/1. It appears from the list of rooms in his 1558 probate inventory that he did not in fact insert the floor.

[8]   Alcock, *People at Home*, p. 58.

[9]   PRO PROB4/25461. The text has been lightly edited to remove repetitive text and Roman numerals have been converted to Arabic.

[10]   This reconstruction by Dr Pat Hughes was originally published in M Locock (ed.), *Meaningful Architecture: Social Interpretation of Buildings*, Avebury, 1994.

[11]   Other inventories suggest that a fairly small farm like this one would not have had more than £1-2 worth of cheese at any time.

[12]   As a result, the annual estate rentals do not give a clear picture of who lived in the house in the first half of the nineteenth century.

[13]   SBTRO DR671/104/1 (1813 survey); DR18/31/53ff (annual rentals); DR18/31/711 (1854 survey).

Further Reading and Resources

LOCAL HISTORY: GENERAL SOURCES

Joy Bristow, *The Local Historian's Glossary and Vade Mecum*, University of Nottingham, 1994

David Hey, *The Oxford dictionary of local and family history*, Oxford University Press, 1997

W G Hoskins, *The Making of the English Landscape*, Hodder and Stoughton, 1988 (revised edition with additional material by Christopher Taylor)

W B Stephens, *Sources for English local history* Phillimore, 1994 (3rd edition)

Kate Tiller, *English Local History: an Introduction*, Alan Sutton, 1992

HISTORICAL STUDIES: GENERAL SOURCES

Christopher Dyer, *Everyday Life in Medieval England*, Hambledon, 1994 and *Standards of living in the later Middle Ages*, Cambridge University Press, 1989

Joan Thirsk (ed.) *Agrarian History of England and Wales*, Cambridge University Press (several volumes)

SOURCES FOR THE HISTORY AND DEVELOPMENT OF BUILDINGS

D Arnold (ed.), *The Georgian Villa*, Alan Sutton, 1996.

Maurice Barley, *The English farmhouse and cottage*, Routledge, 1961 (and later printings)

Maurice Barley, *Houses and history*, Faber and Faber, 1986.

P S Barnwell and A T Adams, *The House Within: Interpreting Medieval Houses in Kent*, RCHME, 1994. Much wider in its coverage than the title suggests.

R W Brunskill, *Houses and Cottages of Britain*, Gollancz, 1997.

Lyndon F Cave, *The Smaller English House*, Hale, 1981.

Edmund Gray, *The British house : a concise architectural history*, Barrie and Jenkins, 1994.

Jane Grenville, *Medieval Housing*, Leicester University Press, 1997

H Long, *The Edwardian House*, Manchester University Press, 1993.

Eric Mercer, *English Vernacular Houses*, HMSO, 1975

S Muthesius, *The English Terraced House*, Yale University Press, 1982.

Anthony Quiney, *House and home : a history of the small English house*, BBC, 1986 and *The Traditional Buildings of England*, Thames and Hudson, 1990

M Wood, *The English Medieval House*, Bracken Books, 1983 (original edition 1965).

BUILDINGS IN INDIVIDUAL COUNTIES

Victoria County History when available, though the earlier volumes give relatively little information.

Nikolaus Pevsner and co-authors, *Buildings of England*; *Buildings of Scotland*; *Buildings of Wales*. Minor domestic buildings are only given prominence in the later volumes and in revised editions (see, for example the second editions of *Devon* and *Buckinghamshire*).

Listed Buildings: Consult the schedules, held by Planning Departments and usually by County Record Offices. Most of the descriptions are also available on the *Images of England* web-site (below).

GUIDES TO HOUSE HISTORY

D Austin, M Dowdy, and J Miller, *Be Your Own House Detective*, BBC, 1997. Mainly a series of case studies, with some major errors. The brief section on documents does not describe how to find them or to study them systematically.

Nick Barratt, *House History Starter Pack*, Public Record Office, 2002. Includes check sheets to help organise the research.

Nick Barratt, *Tracing the history of your house*, Public Record Office, 2001. Mainly restricted to sources in the PRO.

Bill Breckon and Jeffery Parker (revised by Martin Andrew), *Tracing the History of Houses*, Countryside Books, 2000. Essentially an architectural guide with only two pages on documents.

Peter Bushell, *Tracing the History of your House*, Pavilion, 1989. Clear architectural summary but the documentary information is very general and mainly genealogical in emphasis.

Pamela Cunnington, *How Old is Your House?* Marston House, 1999.

David Iredale and John Barrett, *Discovering your old house*, Shire Publications, 2002. A good general survey.

GUIDES TO PALAEOGRAPHY, LATIN AND DATING

E A Gooder, *Latin for Local History*, Longmans, 1978.

C R Cheney, *Handbook of Dates for Students of English History*, Cambridge University Press, 2000.

H E Grieve, *Examples of English Handwriting, 1150-1750*, Essex Record Office, 1954 and later editions.

L C Hector, *The Handwriting of English Documents*, reprinted Kohler and Coombes, 1980.

Alf Ison, *A Secretary Hand ABC Book*, Berkshire Books, 1982 (obtainable from Berkshire Record Office). The best short guide to Tudor and Stuart handwriting.

H Jenkinson, *The Later Court Hands in England from the 15th to the 17th Century*, Cambridge University Press, 1927. This and the following are full sources for reference.

C Johnson and H Jenkinson, *English Court Hand, A.D. 1066-1500*, Cambridge University Press, 1915

C T Martin, *The Record Interpreter*, reprinted Phillimore & Co., 1982.

K C Newton, *Medieval Land Records: A Reading Aid*, Historical Association, 1971.

Denis Stuart, *Latin for Local and Family Historians*, Phillimore & Co., 1995.

GUIDES TO DOCUMENTARY SOURCES

N W Alcock, *Old Title Deeds*, 2nd ed., Phillimore, 2001.

A J Camp, *Wills and their whereabouts*, the author, 1974.

J Gibson and C Rogers, *Electoral Registers since 1832 and Burgess Rolls*, Federation of Family History Societies, 1990.

J Gibson and C Rogers, *Poll Books c. 1696-1872: a directory to holdings in Great Britain*, Federation of Family History Societies, 1994.

MAPS

W E Tate, *Domesday of English Enclosure Acts and Awards*, University of Reading, 1978.

J Chapman, *A guide to Parliamentary Enclosures in Wales*, University of Wales Press,1992.

Public Record Office, *Maps and Plans in the Public Record Office: Vol. 1, British Isles c. 1410-1860*, 1967.

B Short, *Land and society in Edwardian Britain*, Cambridge University Press, 1997. Comprehensive examination of the 1910 Domesday.

TAX ASSESSMENTS

J Gibson, M Medlycott and D Mill (eds), *Land and Window Tax assessments 1690-1950*, Federation of Family History Societies, 1997.

M Turner, & D Mills, (eds) *Land and Property: The English Land Tax, 1692-1832*, Alan Sutton, 1986.

J Gibson, *Hearth Tax Returns and other later Stuart Tax Lists and the Association Oath Rolls*, Federation of Family History Societies, 1996.

SOCIAL HISTORY AND LIFESTYLE

N W Alcock, *People at Home*, Phillimore, 1993

Philip Ariés and Georges Duby (eds), *A History of Private Life*, Belknap Press, 1987-92, esp. vols 2-4. A French bias, but significant English content.

L Weatherill, *Consumer behaviour and material culture in Britain, 1660-1760*, Routledge, 1988.

VERNACULAR ARCHITECTURE BIBLIOGRAPHIES

For documentary sources, see Section VIII in each volume. Volumes III and IV of these bibliographies are available on-line at: *http://ads.ahds.ac.uk/catalogue/* [click on Library].

R de Z Hall, *A Bibliography on Vernacular Architecture, [Volume I]*, David & Charles, 1972

D J H Michelmore (ed.), *A Supplementary Bibliography of Vernacular Architecture, [Volume II], 1970-1976*, Vernacular Architecture Group, 1979

I R Pattison, D S Pattison and N W Alcock (eds.), *A Bibliography of Vernacular Architecture, Volume III, 1977-1989*, Vernacular Architecture Group, 1992

I R Pattison, D S Pattison and N W Alcock (eds.), *A bibliography of Vernacular Architecture, Volume IV, 1990-1994*, Vernacular Architecture Group, 1999

ON-LINE GUIDES AND RESOURCES

National Register of Archives   *www.nra.gov.uk*

Public Record Office   *www.pro.gov.uk.*
    In its Information Section, this includes a list of sources for house history with links
    to house history sites for individual counties. See also the PRO On-line Catalogue
    (PROCAT).

Land Registry   *www.landreg.gov.uk*

General house history   *www.jams.swinternet.co.uk*
    The emphasis is on the physical structure more than documentary resources.

The Builder (vols 1-10)   *www.bodley.ox.ac.uk/ilej/*

GENEALOGICAL ON-LINE SOURCES

International Genealogical Index   *www.familysearch.org*

Free Births Marriages & Deaths   *freebmd.rootsweb.com*

IMAGE SOURCES

British Architectural Library, Royal Institute of British Architects, 66 Portland Place,
    London W1B 1AD (on-line catalogue accessible via *site.yahoo.net/riba-library*)

England: National Monuments Record Centre, Great Western Village, Kemble Drive,
    Swindon SN2 2GZ (*www.english-heritage.org.uk*)

Images of England: on-line descriptions and images of buildings listed as of architectural
    and historical importance (maintained by National Monuments Record):
    www.imagesofengland.org.uk

Northern Ireland: Monuments and Buildings Record, 5-33 Hill Street, Belfast BT1 2LA,
    Northern Ireland (*www.ehsni.gov.uk/built/mbr/mbr.shtml*)

Scotland: National Monuments Record of Scotland, John Sinclair House, 16 Bernard
    Terrace, Edinburgh, EH8 9NX (*www.rcahms.gov.uk*)

Wales: Royal Commission on the Ancient and Historical Monuments of Wales, Plas Crug,
    Aberystwyth, Ceredigion, Wales SY23 1NJ (*www.rcahmw.org.uk/nmrw.shtml*)

Eire: Irish Architectural Archive, 73 Merrion Square Dublin 2 (*www.iarc.ie*)

ORGANISATIONS

Ancient Monuments Society, St Ann's Vestry Hall, 2 Church Entry, London EC4V 5HB
    (*www.ancientmonumentssociety.org.uk*)

Georgian Group, 6 Fitzroy Square, London W1T 5DX (*www.georgiangroup.org.uk*)

The Society for the Protection of Ancient Buildings, 37 Spital Square, London E1 6DY
    (*www.spab.org.uk*)

Vernacular Architecture Group, c/o Cathy Groves, Archaeology Research School, Sheffield
    University, 2 Mappin Street, Sheffield S1 4DT (*www.vag.org.uk*)

The Victorian Society, 1 Priory Gardens, Bedford Park, London W4 1TT
    (*www.victorian-society.org.uk*)

General Index

1909-10 Domesday, *see* Finance Act (1909-10)

Abstracts of Title, 29

Abuttals, 35

Acock's Green, Birmingham, 21

Acts, 1922 Law of Property, 33

    2002 Land Registration, 27
    see also Finance Act (1909-10)

Addyngton, Thomas, 65

Advertisements, 60f

Aleyn, Peter, 98

Alscot, Warwickshire, 69, 83

Aston Cantlow, Warwickshire, 22, 86

Aston Somerville, Gloucestershire, 86

Atherstone-on-Stour, Warwickshire, 69f

Austen, Jane, 62

Austin, Henry Edward, 81

Bankruptcy papers, 63

Barnethurst (Branthurst): Alice, 75f; Robert, 75f; Thomas, 75f; William, 75f

Bath, Somerset, 3, 31

    expiration of 99-year leases, 31

Bay window, 65

Bedfordshire, 59

Best, Mary Ellen, 59

Birmingham, 20f, 26, 42; Acock's Green, 21; Edgbaston, 43

Black Death, 63

Blacksmiths Guild of Coventry, 93

Blake, Arthur, 81

Borough property, 21

Bounty, Queen Anne's, 53f

Bowhill Manor, Exeter, Devon, 30

Breconshire, 26

Brett, Charles, 81

Bristol, 5

British Architectural Library, 5

Broadley, Emma, 81; Richard, 80f

Buckinghamshire, 53

Buckler family drawings, 59

Builders, 1

Builders' records, 55, 66

Building, accounts, 56

    contracts, 56, 64

    evidence, 41

    finances, 80

    leases, 31, 78

    plans, 42; Local Authority, 56

Buller, William, 85

Bullock, John, 69

Burt, John and Mary Ann, 80f

Cale, William, 89

Camill (Campbell):; Elizabeth, 94f; Holloway, 94f; Mary, 94f; Richard, 94ff; Sarah, 94f; Thomas, 94f, 98

Campbell *see* Camill

Canal buildings, 36

Carr, Charles John, 81

Casmore, Francis, 96

Catesby, Ann and John, 74ff

Census, 80, 86